BEGINNING
OF THE
END

BEGINNING OF THE

The Assassination of
Yitzhak Rabin and the
Coming Antichrist

JOHN HAGEE

Thomas Nelson Publishers
Nashville • Atlanta • London • Vancouver

Published in Nashville, Tennessee, by Thomas Nelson, Inc., Publishers, and distributed in Canada by Word Communications, Ltd., Richmond, British Columbia, and in the United Kingdom by Word (UK), Ltd., Milton Keynes, England.

Unless otherwise noted, all Scripture quotations are from the New King James Version of the Bible, © 1979, 1980, 1982, 1984 by Thomas Nelson, Inc., Publishers.

Scripture quotations noted NIV are taken from the HOLY BIBLE, NEW INTERNATIONAL VERSION®. Copyright © 1973, 1978, 1984 by International Bible Society. Used by permission of Zondervan Bible Publishing House. All rights reserved.

The "NIV" and "New International Version" trademarks are registered in the United States Patent and Trademark Office by International Bible Society. Use of either trademark requires the permission of International Bible Society.

Scripture quotations noted NASB are from THE NEW AMERICAN STANDARD BIBLE, Copyright © 1960, 1962, 1963, 1968, 1971, 1972, 1973, 1975, 1977 by The Lockman Foundation and are used by permission.

ISBN 0–7852-7370-0

Printed in the United States of America

5 6 7 — 00 99 98 97 96

TO MY MOTHER AND FATHER,

Reverend Bythel Hagee and Vada Swick Hagee,
whose love of God's Word
has been the guiding force in my life.

Table of Contents

Introduction

For hundreds and even thousands of years, Christians and Jews have been looking for their Messiah. To the Jewish people, the Messiah has yet to come. To Christians, He has already come and will come again.

I am writing this book because I want you to know that the coming of the Messiah is not a theory for scholars to debate. It is not a fable for the sophisticated to ignore. It is not a factoid for the fastidious to file. It is not a riddle for the obsessive to solve. It is instead the most important truth of our age—not merely to understand but to anticipate, embrace, and live out.

I believe this not only because of my unshakable confidence in what the Bible says about the future, but also because the events of these last months draw me inexorably to the conclusion that the Messiah is coming very soon. And no other event in recent history underscores this more than the assassination of one of the greatest men of our age—Yitzhak Rabin.

I'm writing this book to help you see how the events of recent days fit into God's accelerating prophetic timetable for the world, Israel, and you. But I want you to do more than just see the outline—I want you to grasp the outcome. I want this book to be a wake-up call to you that the prophesied events are fast approaching and will affect you!

With every tick of the clock, the prophecies of the Word of God come closer and closer to fruition. This is not just an intriguing coincidence—it is an irrefutable demonstration that God is in complete control over all of human history. God's will is going to be accomplished. His victory is going to be complete. As you're reading this book, I want you to ask yourself whether the God who controls history controls you? Have you yielded fully to His sovereignty? Or are you a speed bump God will roll over as He brings His Word to pass?

I'm also writing this book to help you understand that tomorrow might not be like today. This evening might not be like this morning. The next hour might not be like this hour. There is absolutely no guarantee that tomorrow will be like today, and I hope this book will make that fact very clear. There is a tomorrow that will usher in events that will completely change this planet and that will radically change your life and your future. This is not the time to put off doing what you know to be right. This is not the time to procrastinate. This is not the time for complacency. This is not the time to be lukewarm. This *is* the time to realize that one day time will be no more and the choices you have made in life will be irrevocably ratified for all eternity.

I'm writing this book with three distinct audiences in mind:

- *For Jews:* I am writing as a friend to set before you what God's Word says about the momentous choices Israel and the Jewish people face as you cope with the assassination of Yitzhak Rabin and the prospect and price of peace in the Middle East. I want to show you God's future for Israel and Jerusalem. And I want to share with you what the Word of God says about Messiah's past and His future.

- *For Christians:* I am writing to increase your confidence in God and His Word. What He has predicted will come to pass, and it is happening right before our very eyes. I am writing to bolster your courage—God not only provides, He protects: as we do His work, and from the wrath to come. Now more than ever we need to be strong and courageous—to attempt great things for God and to expect great things from God. The time is short.

• *For those who have missed the Rapture:* I am writing to the one who finds this book in the future time of Tribulation. You may be confused and terrified by the momentous events you are experiencing. You may be in hiding. Like so many other books, this book may be contraband. You may feel alone. You may be hungry, thirsty, homeless, and desperately ill. You may ache inside from grieving over the horrific human slaughter—not only in the world as a whole but also among *your* family and *your* friends. You may be tempted to believe the explanation for these events offered by the world leader—explanations that everyone around you seems to believe. Know this: the Word of God has predicted all of these events for centuries. And just as what you're now experiencing was foretold long ago, the Word of God also predicts that all enemies of the Messiah will be conclusively and completely destroyed soon. Read this book and you'll meet the real Messiah. Take heed to this book, then lift up your heads—your redemption draws near.

CHAPTER ONE

The Assassination

Yigal Amir, a young Jewish student who studied law and computers at Tel Aviv's Bar Ilan University, dressed himself carefully. Before leaving his room, he paused for a long moment to stare at his face in the mirror.

The date was Saturday, November 4, 1995—the night Israeli Prime Minister Yitzhak Rabin would attend a peace rally in Tel Aviv.

The large, soulful brown eyes blinked slowly. Twice before, at the Yad Vashem Holocaust Memorial, he had been close to the prime minister, but security had been too tight. The gun had stayed in his pocket, out of sight. But it was ever-ready, loaded with dumdum bullets specially made by Yigal's brother, Hagai. Hagai had hollowed out the noses of the nine-millimeter bullets, making them more lethal. It would only take one . . . when the time came. When the time was right.

He studied his reflection: his mother's eyes, a soft, curling beard like his father's.

Tonight, if God was good, an opportunity would show itself. No longer would Rabin be able to transfer Israeli lands to Palestinians. The damage he'd done in the West Bank and Gaza Strip was enough. Israel had a divine right to the land, and to give it away was an act of treason against Israel and an abomination to God.

Yigal gave his reflection a slow smile, then pulled his jacket over the T-shirt he was wearing and walked out into the street.

Two hours later, he walked through the crowd toward the prime minister's car. He exchanged pleasantries with a policeman who did not seem in the least suspicious. The security men were looking for Arab assassins; they did not appear to care about the knot of young Jewish men who huddled near the armored vehicle.

Amir loitered near the car, once even exchanging a quick smile with a bodyguard who must have taken him for a driver.

He ducked behind a large potted plant and pulled the gun from his pocket. Cold. Heavy in his hand. A good weapon for the defense of Israel and the will of God.

The crowd stirred, and Rabin walked toward Amir, his head bobbing as he spoke with a man to his left.

Yigal stretched out his arm and squeezed the trigger of the 9mm Beretta. Point blank range. Someone was shouting, "It's nothing! It's nothing!" and Yigal was amazed to realize the voice was his own.

Rabin and a wounded bodyguard collapsed into the car as strong hands seized Yigal's shoulders and arms. Someone wrenched the gun from his hands; other hands forced him to the ground, where he felt the asphalt against his cheek.

Screams. Shouts. Exhilaration.

"I acted alone on God's orders, and I have no regrets," he whispered, his breath stirring the dirt on the road. He whispered the line again, practicing. Soon he would tell the world why. For now, he was content to let the world discover what he'd done.

Yitzhak Rabin, the Warrior Statesman

The world reeled in shock and grief when the hand of hatred assassinated Prime Minister Rabin of Israel. It was not a kaffiyeh-wearing Arab terrorist who had committed this heinous crime. It was another Jew.

Yitzhak Rabin was a warrior statesman whose masterful organization of the Israeli Defense Forces in 1967 led to the absolute demolition of the enemies of Israel. He was an old soldier who could be very tough with the Palestinians; they knew he was a man of action.

Yet he was equally a man of peace. He was not a dreamy-eyed idealist reaching for the impossible peace accord between ancient enemies. He was a veteran statesman with nerves of steel, pursuing the treasure of peace so coveted by Israel.

The world mourned his passing. World leaders gathered around his coffin at Jerusalem's Mount Herzl cemetery.

Egypt's President Hosni Mubarak and King Hussein of Jordan paid tribute to the man who had led Israel against them in 1967.

Bill Clinton, George Bush, and Jimmy Carter were among those representing the United States; British Prime Minister John Major, German Chancellor Helmut Kohl, and French President Jacques Chirac also attended.

Representatives of six Arab states and the Palestinian Authority attended the funeral, most of whom were visiting the homeland of their ancient enemies for the first time. Reuters NewMedia reported, "The presence of officials from so many Arab states, and from Israel's former arch-enemy, the Palestine Liberation Organization, would have been unthinkable just three years ago when Rabin took office."[1]

Yassir Arafat, chairman of the Palestine Liberation Organization, watched the funeral on television and later visited Rabin's widow and offered his condolences. "I am hoping God will help us to continue our very difficult march and the peace process," he said.

Acting Israeli Prime Minister Shimon Peres said, "We are determined to continue the peace process."

And Leah Rabin, the assassinated leader's widow, told a crowd outside her home, "I think the cold-blooded murder of this man, who made such a gigantic contribution to the peace process, will shock many people and perhaps . . . be a turning point in the public conscience."[2] I believe her words will prove to be prophetic.

But the speaker who tugged on the world's heartstrings was Noa Ben-Artzi Philosof, Rabin's eighteen-year-old grand-daughter. Choking back tears, she stood before a sea of television cameras and quietly asked the angels to protect him. "Great men have already eulogized you but no one has felt, like I have, the caress of your warm and soft hands, or your warm embrace which was reserved for us alone and your half-smile which always told me so much. That same smile is no more and froze with you," she said. "We love you, grandfather, forever."[3] The world listened and wept.

After returning from Rabin's funeral, Southern Baptist Convention President Jim Henry said, "This [assassination] will galvanize [world leaders] for the immediate future to press on with it. [Rabin's] death made people realize, in a sense, what peace costs. And they want to move on with it; they want to get something done. He was the cement, the glue in the process, and how that plays out in the long run will be interesting."[4]

Interesting? Very—I believe the instant that Yigal Amir pulled the trigger will stand as a defining moment in world history.

Memories of Rabin

I met Prime Minister Rabin on a number of occasions—when he was the prime minister and when he was not. Typically, most people who met him first noticed a certain shyness about him, but after several minutes of conversation his warmth and brilliance would reveal themselves.

Our first meeting was the most memorable. My wife, Diana, and I were at the Westin Hotel in Houston where Israel Bonds, a Jewish fund-raising group, was hosting a dinner intended to raise money for the state of Israel.

Cornerstone Church in San Antonio, where I serve as pastor, has been producing an event called "The Night to Honor Israel" since 1981, so we were invited to the Israel Bonds dinner, which was attended by the who's who of Houston's Jewish community.

Diana and I were thrilled to be part of the evening, so we flew from San Antonio to Houston and took a taxi to the Westin Hotel. We were early. Outside the banquet hall, Yitzhak Rabin was standing near the door with representatives of the Israel Bonds.

I was formally introduced to the future prime minister by Bob Abrams, the director of Israel Bonds. I extended my hand, and Rabin shook it warmly and asked me, "What is 'The Night to Honor Israel'?"

"It is an event inspired while I was praying at the Western Wall in Jerusalem in the spring of 1978," I answered. "It was my first time in Israel, and I felt a very special presence in the city of Jerusalem. Somehow, I felt Jerusalem was my spiritual home."

Rabin listened thoughtfully, so I went on. "As I prayed at the Wall, a Jewish man dressed in his prayer shawl and yarmulke was praying next to me, bowing and kissing his prayer book. As I watched him pray, I realized I knew very little about my Jewish roots as a Christian. From that moment I have felt divinely inspired to bring Christians and Jews together in a public arena to celebrate the things we have in common, to honor the nation of Israel, and to combat anti-Semitism."

Rabin cocked his head sideways, looked me straight in the eye for at least ten seconds without saying a word. *Is he going to answer me?* I wondered.

Finally he gave me that world famous half-smile and said, "That's good. Thank you, Pastor, for your help."

Diana and I entered the magnificent banquet hall and located our table. I have been to legions of banquets, but this was one of the most lavish I have ever attended. A two-tiered dais with about thirty people on each tier was situated at the front of the room: the movers and shakers of Houston.

My wife and I were the only Gentiles present.

After a kosher meal and delightful conversation, Yitzhak Rabin was introduced, and the statesman gave an update on conditions in Israel and the state of the American-Israeli relationship. He spoke very slowly in a deep, stentorian voice that captivated the audience. His analysis of world conditions was brilliant, and his points were well-reasoned.

After Rabin's speech, Billy Goldberg, chairman of the event, took the microphone. Billy is a bottom-line, cut-to-the-chase kind of guy. He announced that to save time, every table should select a spokesperson to announce the gifts to Israel Bonds that each individual would make.

At that moment I felt perspiration forming on my brow.

Then Billy Goldberg took my breath away by declaring that he was going to give $250,000. He pointed to one of his associates and said, "And he's going to give $250,000."

Thank you, God, that Billy doesn't know me!

Every person on the dais made their pledges—huge, unbelievable sums. Then the attention turned to the people on the main floor of the banquet hall. The smallest pledge made at the first two tables was $25,000—offered by a little Jewish lady, clutching her purse tightly.

Diana leaned over and whispered, "John, I think she has the money in her purse!"

I looked back at her and asked one of the most stupid questions of my adult life: "Did you bring the checkbook?"

She looked at me and laughed out loud. When she had regained her composure, she whispered, "What difference does that make?" she answered, smiling. "You can have every check in the book, but there's nothing in the bank." At that point our church was much smaller and our finances were tighter than the bark on a tree.

Panic time. We were at the third table and it was time to declare what we would give. I was looking around, thinking I could fake a heart attack and have Diana carry me out.

I told Diana we would find one thousand dollars somewhere, even if we had to go to the bank and borrow it. Meekly and in the most muffled voice I could manage, I told the captain of our table that Diana and I would be giving one thousand dollars.

He blinked, then said, "Would you mind repeating that?" And so, my face burning, I said it again: "A thousand dollars." It felt like so little; I wanted the floor to open up and just swallow me whole.

I was totally unprepared for what happened next. The captain of our table announced with thunderous delight to the entire banquet hall: "Reverend and Mrs. Hagee will be giving one thousand dollars."

The next moment was an eternity. Dead silence filled the banquet hall. I wanted to disappear, not knowing what they were thinking of us, but imagining all sorts of things . . . all of them negative.

At that moment Yitzhak Rabin's face shifted into a half-smile, and he began to clap, slowly, methodically, rhythmically. Startled, I looked up at him, then the entire room exploded into applause. The other guests rose to their feet, still clapping, and I grabbed Diana's hand and looked at the floor, my face as red as a ruby. A standing ovation for one thousand dollars?

What I had imagined as a small gift was appreciated in Rabin's eyes. Gratitude poured from my heart because he approved of two Gentiles who didn't have a lot to give but who were concerned for Israel.

I was never more embarrassed in all my life and never received more recognition for giving a thousand dollars. But I'll always be grateful to Yitzhak Rabin for a memory of warmth and kindness that I'll treasure for life.

Peace at Any Price

The shot that killed Yitzhak Rabin launched Bible prophecy onto the fast track. Why?

In order to understand the reasons behind the assassination, we must first understand Israel's recent history. Listen to Rabbi Eliezer Waldman as he explains how and why many Israelis were frustrated with the West Bank Accord that was recently signed at the White House: "Our government went behind the back of the people to meet secretly, against the law, with the PLO," he says. "It pushed through legislation which made profound and dangerous changes in Israeli policy, changes which clearly affected the security of the nation. With the barest majority of the government, and, very possibly, against the majority of the people, it agreed to give away vital parts of our homeland. And, what is most painful, they agreed to compromise on Jerusalem. It closed all avenues of protest and even excessively punished those who voiced opposition to such changes."[5]

Rabin's assassination came at a time when public opinion of the peace process in Israel was lukewarm at best. The peace accords signed at the White House by Rabin and Arafat stipulated that Israeli troops would withdraw from six major towns in the West Bank, turning them over to Palestinian self-rule after twenty-eight years of occupation. Early surveys showed that public opinion of the West Bank Accord was evenly divided between approval and disapproval, but a Dahaf poll released the week after Rabin's murder indicated that an astounding 74 percent of Israelis believed the government should continue implementing the Palestinian self-rule accord. And, while in recent polls Labor leader Rabin had trailed his rival, opposition Likud leader Binyamin Netanyahu, the Dahaf survey showed 54 percent would vote for Peres and the Labor party if the election were held today, and only 23 percent for Netanyahu.[6]

The bullets from Yigal Amir's gun shed the blood of a Nobel Peace Prize winner, who was proclaimed a martyr for peace within minutes of his death. His blood will now become the bonding force that will drive the nation of Israel and other leaders of the Middle East to new heights of unity to secure a legacy of peace for Yitzhak Rabin.

"There is nothing else that we can do . . . but to continue a great road paved by a great leader," acting Prime Minister Shimon Peres told reporters after an emergency cabinet meeting within hours of the assassination. "I asked myself if this happened to me, what would I want to happen later," Peres said. "I have one answer—to continue the path of peace."[7]

Jordan's King Hussein, who in 1994 ended forty-six years of hostility with Israel, stood at Rabin's funeral and proclaimed that he hoped to leave behind a legacy of peace when he died. "Standing here, I commit before you," he said, "before my people in Jordan, and before the world, to continue to do our utmost to ensure that we leave a similar legacy. When my time comes, I hope it will be like my grandfather's and like Yitzhak Rabin's."[8]

United States President Bill Clinton urged the Middle Eastern countries toward peace. "Your prime minister was a martyr for peace," he said. "Surely we must learn from his martyrdom. . . . Now it falls to all of us who love peace and all of us who loved him to carry on the struggle to which he gave life and for which he gave his life."[9]

In November 1994, I was touring Israel with three hundred American Zionists, a mixture of Jews and Gentiles who support Israel. After a long day of seeing the historical sites, I had gone to my hotel room. I was tired and nearly asleep, but I was brought wide awake by an unexpected knock at my door.

I looked through the peephole in the door and recognized a friend of mine who was an orthodox rabbi. He had three strangers with him, two men and a woman, but I trusted him. So I put on my robe, opened the door, and let them in.

"Can we talk to you?" they asked. After introducing themselves and telling me they were Israeli journalists, they said, "We want to tell you what's going on in Israel with regard to the peace process."

Each one of them gave a similar testimony, but one thing became very clear: any journalist who said anything negative about the peace process did so at the risk of his career. Such a journalist ceased to be invited to government press conferences. Not only were they taken "out of the loop" professionally, but the government of Israel was placing in ninety-day detention any individual who said or did anything to discredit the peace process publicly. They told me that the democratic process had been totally derailed in Israel. People were picked up at all hours of the night and day for questioning. Anyone who was in any way critical of the peace process was subject to governmental harassment.

That happened before the assassination and Rabin's martyrdom. Now that the mood of the people has gone into the euphoric dimension of "peace at any price," the situation will be even more intense to guarantee the success of the peace movement.

The journalists told me, "You are on national television in America, you speak to millions of people, and at some point we want you to let the American people know how the democratic process here is being scrubbed in a fanatical pursuit of peace. We want you to know how intensely the government is pressing this peace issue. The authorities are abandoning the democratic procedure for which Israel is so very well known. There are things being done in the name of peace that threaten the security of Israel, but if we write about those things, we will never be invited to another press conference and we could lose our jobs or go to jail."

What was once a political operation has blossomed into a national mandate, created by the blood of a martyr.

The Mountain Moves: Syria Is Willing to Negotiate

Israel had treaties with Egypt and Jordan prior to the Rabin assassination and had signed an accord with the PLO. But Syria, a dominant player in the Middle East, has never been able to come to terms with Israel because at the heart of the Syrian-Israeli dispute is the strategic Golan Heights. Israel captured this region from Syria in the 1967 Middle East War and later annexed it.

The Golan Heights, a strategic plateau overlooking northern Israel and the southern Syrian plains, is critical both militarily and as a watershed (see map on page 12). The area is a towering plateau which measures about 480 square miles and is distinguished by two levels; the Lower Golan in the south, with altitudes between 600 and 1,900 feet, and the Upper Golan in the north, rising to altitudes of up to 3,000 feet above sea level. A number of hilltops reach as high as 4,400 feet.

This lofty platform is the perfect place from which to launch rockets to reach Jerusalem. Israel lies at the base of the Golan Heights. One guiding principle in warfare is to "take the high ground": whoever owns the Golan Heights could make all of Israel a killing field.

Never before has Israel even hinted that it might be willing to negotiate on issues regarding the Golan Heights, but now, in the words of Warren Christopher, United States Secretary of State, Israel and Syria will open a "new phase" of intensive and broad peace negotiations. Though two previous attempts to open talks on security issues collapsed in the past year, Christopher says there is a "new mood" in Israel since Rabin's assassination.[10]

Upon taking office on November 22, Peres said, "I would like to propose to the president of Syria that we each do our utmost to put an end to the era of wars in the Middle East."

He has declared that he is open to any form of negotiations with no preconditions. The *New York Times* reports that Israeli news reports speculate that Peres would be prepared to return virtually all of the Golan in exchange for firm security and a comprehensive Mideast peace.[11]

GOLAN HEIGHTS

(Aerial View)

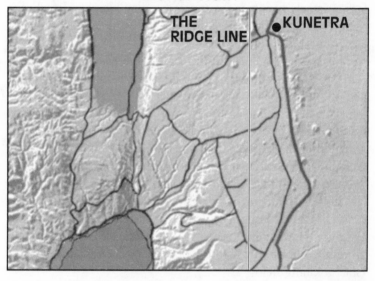

(Elevation View)

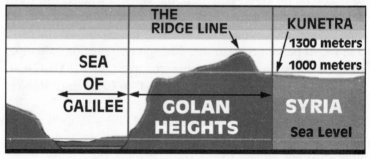

The Assassination's Prophetic Significance

In the surge of advocates for peace, voices of dissent will be shouted down or ignored. The peace process will cease to become a political action; it will become a spiritual mandate for a nation.

Based on the words of the prophets of Israel, I believe this peace process will lead to the most devastating war Israel has ever known. After that war, the longed-for Messiah will come. This book was written to reveal how the peace process will likely develop and the reasons for a war over the three-thousand-year-old city of Jerusalem.

Several months ago, someone asked me, "Dr. Hagee, your father was a prophecy scholar, and you have followed in his footsteps. Do you believe the Arabs will ever gain a sufficient foothold in Israel to birth a Palestinian state or gain control of a portion of the city of Jerusalem?"

Ten years ago, no one could imagine such a thing ever happening. Israel is the fourth-greatest military power on the face of the earth; they have defeated the combined Arab armies on several occasions. Israel is the dominant military force in the Middle East, and no one reasonably believes that the Arab nations could ever defeat them. But the prophecies of Scripture indicate the Arabs will gain a foothold in the Middle East sufficient enough to convince them they can defeat Israel in a war.

Think back with me to September 19, 1993. Israeli Prime Minister Rabin stood in the White House Rose Garden House with Yasser Arafat. President Clinton stood between them, eager to announce that Rabin and Arafat had, the previous day, signed the West Bank accord. At that signing, Rabin had declared that the land flowing with milk and honey should not become a land flowing with blood and tears.

Now on public display, the world watched and waited as the peace accord was announced. Would the warrior statesman who masterminded the 1967 war shake hands with Arafat the terrorist, the man who had engineered murderous attacks on buses, retirement homes, and orphanages? And would Arafat take the hand of his sworn enemy?

At a dramatic moment, Arafat extended his hand in friendship and Yitzhak Rabin shook it before the cameras of the world. Some saw it and wept. Others applauded. Others saw it as an act of treason against the state of Israel and began to call for the expulsion of Yitzhak Rabin as Prime Minister. Others watched and grimly decided that Rabin deserved to die.

Yigal Amir saw it and believed that Rabin was a traitor to the Jewish cause. "The entire nation did not pay attention to the fact that a Palestinian state was being created," Amir told an Israeli court after his arrest. "I did not try to stop the peace process because there is no such concept. . . . I was at the demonstration. It was fifty percent Arabs. What will you do when there are two million Arabs here? Will we give the state to the Arabs?"[12]

The question now being asked around the world and in the halls of Congress is: "Will this assassination slow down the peace process or speed it up?" We can find the answer in our own American history books.

In the months prior to John F. Kennedy's assassination, very little of his party's legislation passed in Congress. But after JFK's murder, when Lyndon Baines Johnson went to the White House, virtually everything Johnson urged forward in Kennedy's name sailed through both houses of Congress. Johnson himself was elected president in 1964 by the largest majority ever at that time.

Now Israel faces a similar situation. The nation is uniting; all Israel will now pursue peace with a passion that throws caution to the wind. To honor the life and memory of Yitzhak Rabin, Israel will pursue peace with dogged determination.

CHAPTER TWO

The Mind of an Assassin

Yigal Amir, Rabin's murderer, is the second of eight children. His father works as a scribe who handwrites holy Scriptures, his mother, as a nursery school teacher. Yigal Amir had worked abroad as an envoy for an Israeli government agency. He had no police record. Nothing in his family life suggested that he might pick up a gun and murder his country's prime minister. Why did he do it?

Amir told a Jerusalem court that he was required to kill Rabin because the prime minister was handing over parts of the West Bank to Palestinians, a step Amir believed would lead to war and the loss of Jewish life. Therefore, said the assassin, Rabin was a would-be murderer, and under Jewish law intended to allow for self-defense, it is permissible to kill such a person. Outside Jewish Orthodoxy, nearly everyone disagrees with Amir's understanding of that law. Yet within Orthodoxy, a minority supports it.[1]

The Israeli government interrogated two rabbis who were suspected of authorizing, approving, or inspiring Yigal Amir. Authorities believe that the rabbis may have branded Rabin a traitor or *rodef,* the ancient term for a pursuer who is about to kill a Jew. Under Halacha, or Jewish law, it is permissible to kill a *rodef.*[2]

"That this centuries-old concept has emerged in the investigation underscores a deep schism between the religious Zionist view of Israel as a biblical homeland given to the Hebrews by God and a more secular vision of Israel as a modern, democratic state," says Storer Rowley, a writer for the *Chicago Tribune*.[3]

"There's a deep spiritual battle, a cultural war, going on as to what Jewish tradition is about," said Rabbi David Hartman, founder-director of the Shalom Hartman Institute for Judaic Studies in Jerusalem. "And the nature of this people and the future of Israel depends on how this battle is going to be fought."[4]

It is important to understand that although there are many groups of Jews in Israel, most can be divided into two categories. One category is composed of religious Jews who believe, among other things, that Israel has a holy deed to the land. The other group is made up of cultural or ethnic Jews who place no great importance on the religious beliefs of the Jewish people. This second group believes the destiny of the Israeli nation must be accomplished through the political process. They seek a young, modern, prosperous nation with an economy based on technology and tourism. Like so many others in the twentieth century, they place more faith in man than in the God of their fathers. And, having no firsthand experience with a pogrom or mass genocide, they are weary of war.

"For the generation of Israelis who can remember the 1948 war for independence, the idealized image of their Israel was the sun-bronzed kibbutznik with a shovel in one hand and a rifle in the other," says Tom Hundley, a writer for the *Chicago Tribune*. "For the generation who came of age after the 1967 Six-Day War that brought Israel the West Bank, the kibbutznik was replaced by the settler, Bible in one hand, rifle in the other."[5]

Sadly enough, Rabin's assassination may dissuade the second group of Jewish people from seeking to know more about their religious faith. According to Noam M. M. Neusner, a Jewish writer watching the American scene, Amir's murderous act "threatens to undermine a nascent movement in the mainstream American Jewish community toward religion. People now recognize that for Judaism to survive, it must matter more than ethnicity, politics and culture, which have predominated for 300 years. For the first time in their history, American Jews were turning to Judaism for guidance on issues beyond ritualistic nit-picking."[6]

Did Amir push that train off the tracks? Perhaps.

Modern Israel

In Tel Aviv today you can find restaurants offering shrimp, ham, and goose liver in cream sauce; not exactly a kosher cuisine, since Jewish law forbids the eating of shellfish, pork, and organ meats. Today's Israeli citizen shops in Tel Aviv for Gucci, Gaultier, and Donna Karan. The economy is booming; per capita income is nearly $17,000—about the same as Britain's and more than double what it was in the seventies. A new Israeli-made soap opera features the opulent lifestyle of the fictional Linowitz family and their relentless pursuit of sex and money.[7]

"I would say the country is in great danger of losing its Jewish soul," Orthodox Rabbi David Hartman told *Newsweek*. "There is a great danger that Israel will be swept up by the MTV-Madonna culture."[8]

Political Jews are not looking for the coming of the Messiah. Menachem Begin, a former prime minister of Israel, was a devout Jew who read the Scripture every day, prayed regularly, quoted the Word of God in his speeches, and openly declared that Israel had a holy mandate to exist and to possess *eretz yisrael,* the Land of Israel. But Menachem Begin now belongs to the ages, and Israel's current leaders care more for political processes than for religious tenets and convictions.

Liberal Zionism, according to Zeev Sternhell, a professor of political science at Hebrew University, is "a recognition of the fact that Israel is more than a Jewish state, that it belongs also to the 20 percent of its citizens who are Arab. . . . What counts are the universal values, the Rights of Man, and not the particularist Jewish values of Judaism."[9]

The United States has been waging a similar struggle—have we wandered far from the Judeo-Christian ideals upon which we were founded and, if so, should we return? But our struggle has been somewhat diluted by the sheer size and diversity of our country. Israel is a smaller place, surrounded by hostile neighbors for most of its history; passions flare higher because the land at stake is more rare, more precious. When they tried to trade land for peace with Egypt in the seventies, then Prime Minister Golda Meir said, "Israel has no more land to give!"

Many religious Israelis are motivated by a biblical imperative to redeem the land of Israel for the Jews and usher in the coming Messiah. The leading rabbis from Israel and the Diaspora held a conference at the Ramada Renaissance Hotel in Jerusalem in November 1993. Among the resolutions approved at that meeting were the following declarations:

> The assembly restates the fact that the Jewish People are the only legitimate owners of the Land of Israel. This right to the land derives from the promise that God made to the nation's forefathers, and from the unbroken connection of our people to our land throughout the generations even after we were forcibly exiled from it. Through the power of this faith and this connection we returned to the land with the consent of the nations by the monumental decision of the U.N. We reconquered the historic heartland of the land during the Six Day War which was the revelation of Hashem's salvation of His people, a miracle witnessed by the whole world. [*Hashem* is Hebrew for "the name," the sacred four-letter name of God which is never spoken or written.]
>
> The assembly of Rabbis declares that according to the laws of the Torah it is forbidden to relinquish the political rights of sovereignty and national ownership over any part of historic Eretz Yisroel to another authority or people. All of the historic Eretz Yisroel which is now in our possession belongs to the

entire Jewish people past, present and future, and therefore no one in any generation can give away that to which he does not have title. Therefore any agreement to do so is null and void, obligates no one, has no legal or moral force whatsoever.

The assembly calls on the government to fulfill their pledge that no settlement will be dismantled. . . .

The assembly expresses its fear that the "agreement" will endanger the lives of all the inhabitants of Israel, and in particular the lives of those living in Judea, Samaria, and Gaza. The arming of an Arab police force made up of murderous terrorists will be a direct danger in and of itself. . . . Anyone who fails to act in order to prevent the execution of the "agreement" transgresses the sin of "Do not stand still while your neighbor's life is in danger."

We are extremely concerned over the present trend that aims to create a secular culture here which is to blend into "a new Middle East"—a trend which will lead to assimilation. We have a sacred obligation to strengthen and deepen our people's connection to the Torah and to Jewish tradition as passed down through the generations.

We support the continuation of protests, demonstrations, and strikes within the framework of the law. In addition, we encourage educating and informing the masses in order that they may realize the falseness of this "peace" . . .[10]

The above declarations were made two short years ago, but how times have changed!

Rabin's assassination has added fuel to an already hot fire.

The Sacred Title of Property

Who is right? Who owns the land of Israel? The answer is found in the Word of God and can be traced all the way back to Abraham. God sent an angel to tell Abraham that he would be the father of a great nation: "And behold, the word of the LORD came to him, saying . . . 'one who will come from your own body shall be your heir.' Then He brought him outside and said, 'Look now toward heaven, and count the stars if you are able to number them.' And He said to him, 'So shall your descendants be'" (Gen. 15:4–5).

This was surprising news for Abraham, since his wife was already past menopause and had never borne a child. Abraham's wife thought to help God out a bit, and so she asked Abraham to go into the tent of her Egyptian maid, Hagar, and have a child with her—not an unusual practice in those days.

So Abraham slept with Hagar and Ishmael was conceived and born. Later, just as God had foretold, Abraham's wife did conceive and give birth to a miracle baby, Isaac. The people of Israel are descended from Isaac; the people of the Arab nations descended from Ishmael.

To whom does the land of Israel belong? The greatest political controversy of this century is rooted in this question. The Arabs say the land belongs to them, that they've lived in the land for centuries while the Jewish people were scattered across the globe. But the Jewish people claim that the land has belonged to them from the time of Abraham, when Jehovah God entered into a blood covenant with the "Father of all who believe," Abraham, conveying the Promised Land to the children of Abraham, Isaac, and Jacob forever (see Gen. 15:12–17).

If you've bought a house recently, you know that an abstract of title must trace ownership from the very first owner to the present owner, making sure that there is no lien or other claim on the property. Who was the original owner of the land we call Palestine? The answer is recorded many places in Scripture. In Psalm 24:1, we read "The earth is the LORD's." In Psalm 89:11, "The heavens are Thine." In Leviticus 25:23, "The land moreover shall not be sold permanently, for the land is Mine."

Today in Israel, citizens can't own the land; instead they lease it from the government of Israel. If I'm a farmer, I can lease land for forty-nine years, and my son can lease it when my term is done. But neither of us can own it. The land is under the stewardship of the children of Israel, but it ultimately belongs to the Lord. Therefore, God alone can give the land away. When Prime Minister Rabin gave land for peace, religious Jews saw his actions as an attack upon God Himself.

"In the beginning God created the heavens and the earth," we read in Genesis 1:1. God is the Creator/Owner of the earth, and He has the power to confer the title upon whomever He will. In Genesis 12:1 we read that he did transfer title to Abraham, once called Abram : "Now the LORD had said to Abram: 'Get out of your country, from your family and from your father's house, to a land that I will show you.'"

After Abram went to the land God intended, God spoke again to him:

> And the LORD said to Abram, after Lot had separated from him: "Lift your eyes now and look from the place where you are—northward, southward, eastward, and westward; for all the land which you see I give to you and your descendants forever. And I will make your descendants as the dust of the earth; so that if a man could number the dust of the earth, then your descendants also could be numbered. Arise, walk in the land through its length and its width, for I give it to you." (Gen. 13:14–17)

Before Isaac's birth, Abraham asked God if Ishmael might have the royal land grant: "And Abraham said to God, 'Oh, that Ishmael might live before You!'" (Gen. 17:18). In answer, God said he would make Ishmael fruitful, the father of twelve rulers, and a great nation. But God's covenant would be established with Isaac, who was to come. So the title to the land passed from Abraham to Isaac, and eventually, to Jacob.

Isaac was the son of promise, the son of the true wife. Abraham also had six sons with Keturah, the wife he took after Sarah's death. Keturah bore him Zimran, Jokshan, Medan, Midian, Ishbak, and Shuah. These sons became the ancestors

f North Arabian peoples who say, "The land is
n was our father, too!"

am made provision for those sons while he lived.
am gave all that he had to Isaac. But Abraham
gave gu.. ɔ the sons of the concubines which Abraham had;
and while he was still living he sent them eastward, away from
Isaac his son, to the country of the east" (Gen. 25:5–6; see
also 1 Chron. 1:32–33).

God reviewed and reaffirmed his intention to give the land
to Isaac by speaking to him personally.

> Dwell in this land, and I will be with you and bless you; for to
> you and your descendants I give all these lands, and I will per-
> form the oath which I swore to Abraham your father. And I
> will make your descendants multiply as the stars of heaven; I
> will give to your descendants all these lands; and in your seed
> all the nations of the earth shall be blessed; because Abraham
> obeyed My voice and kept My charge, My commandments,
> My statutes, and My laws. (Gen. 26:3–5)

At sixty years of age, Isaac, title holder to what we know
as the Holy Land, discovered that his wife, Rebecca, was ex-
pecting. God performed a sonogram and told Rebecca the
results: "And the LORD said to her: 'Two nations are in your
womb, two peoples shall be separated from your body; one
people shall be stronger than the other, and the older shall
serve the younger'" (Gen. 25:23).

Jacob and Esau emerged from Rebecca's womb. But Esau,
the older twin, did not inherit the title to the land because it
passed to Jacob, to whom his father said, "May God Almighty
bless you, and make you fruitful and multiply you, that you
may be an assembly of peoples; and give you the blessing of
Abraham, to you and your descendants with you, that you
may inherit the land in which you are a stranger, which God
gave to Abraham" (Gen. 28:3–4).

And God Himself confirmed Jacob's ownership of the title when Jacob met God in a dream of a stairway to the stars:

> And behold, the LORD stood above it and said: "I am the LORD God of Abraham your father and the God of Isaac; the land on which you lie I will give to you and your descendants. Also your descendants shall be as the dust of the earth; you shall spread abroad to the west and the east, to the north and the south; and in you and in your seed all the families of the earth shall be blessed." (Gen. 28:13–14; see also Gen. 35:9–12)

And so the title remained with Jacob and his twelve sons. As Joseph, Jacob's beloved son, lay dying in Egypt, he reviewed the title's progression: "And Joseph said to his brethren, 'I am dying; but God will surely visit you, and bring you out of this land to the land of which He swore to Abraham, to Isaac, and to Jacob'" (Gen. 50:24).

How much land is contained within this royal land grant? God Himself has established Israel's boundaries: "On the same day the LORD made a covenant with Abram, saying: 'To your descendants I have given this land, from the river of Egypt to the great river, the River Euphrates'" (Gen. 15:18). The eastern boundary was the Euphrates River, the western boundary the Egyptian River, identified in Exodus 23:31 as the Red Sea. As the children of Israel crossed the Red Sea and left Egypt after the captivity, God said, "Every place on which the sole of your foot treads shall be yours: from the wilderness and Lebanon, from the river, the River Euphrates, even to the Western Sea [the Mediterranean], shall be your territory" (Deut. 11:24). The northern boundary is established in Ezekiel 48:1 as the city of Hamath; the southern boundary is established in Ezekiel 48:28 as the city of Kadesh.

Given these boundaries found in holy Scripture, we discover that Israel will have far more land when Messiah comes than she presently does. Israel's boundaries, established time and

23

time again in the Old Testament, will include all of present-day Israel, all of Lebanon, half of Syria, two-thirds of Jordan, all of Iraq, and the northern portion of Saudi Arabia.

An Ancient Rivalry

The competition that existed in Abraham's household still exists today. The conflict between Arabs and Jews does not involve the West Bank, Judea, or Samaria; it has little to do with the Golan Heights, even though that geographical area is critical to the nation's defense.

The conflict between Arabs and Jews goes deeper than disputes over land. It is theological. It is Judaism versus Islam. Islam's theology insists that Islam triumph over everything else—that's why when you visit an Arabic city, the Islamic prayer tower is the highest point in the city. A follower of Islam is called *Muslim,* a term referring to "one who submits"; the word *Islam* itself literally means "submission." The Arabs believe that while Jesus, Moses, David, and several other Hebrews were prophets, Muhammad was the greatest prophet. Though Muslims revere the Bible, including the Torah, the Psalms, and the Gospels, they hold that the *Al-Quran* (the Koran) is the absolute true word of God, revealed through the angel Jibraeel (Gabriel) to Muhammad. Muslims believe that Allah is God, that he has neither father nor mother, and that he has no sons.

The Muslim Imperative

Did you know that Islam is the fastest growing religion in the United States today?[11] Though most Muslims are peaceful and law-abiding, others have taken advantage of America's civil liberties and have established themselves as "research," "charitable" or "civil rights" institutions. Oliver B. Revell, a former senior FBI official in charge of counterterrorist and counterintelligence investigations, says these groups "are ultimately committed to waging holy war, both in the Middle East and the world at large against all of their opposition."[12]

Seif Ashmawi, an Egyptian-born American-based publisher, agrees. "The aim of these groups," he says, "is the same as their aim in the Middle East: to build and expand their radical religious-political empire and eliminate or discredit all their enemies."[13]

At national conventions sponsored by the Muslim Arab Youth Association (maya), anti-Israeli rhetoric can regularly be heard. At a maya conference held at a Hyatt hotel in Chicago during December 1994, Bassam al-Amoush, a member of the Islamic coalition in the Jordanian parliament, told a joke: "Somebody approached me at the mosque and asked me, 'If I see a Jew in the street, should I kill him?'" Al-Amoush painted on a dumbfounded expression. "'Don't ask me,' I said to him. 'After you kill him, come and tell me.'" The crowd roared with laughter, and al-Amoush continued. "'What do you want from me, a *fatwa* [a religious ruling]? Really, a good deed does not require one.'"[14]

Moments later, journalist Steven Emerson reports, the master of ceremonies held up a note he'd just been handed. "We have very good news," he told the crowd. "There was an attack on a bus in Jerusalem, perpetrated by a Palestinian policeman. Nineteen were wounded and three were killed." The crowd responded with shouts of "Allahu Akbar!"[15]

Why does such enmity exist between the Jews and the Arabs? Much of it probably springs from the ancient rivalry between Isaac and Ishmael. Most of it is due to the fact that the Arab Palestinians feel they have been displaced by Israel. They certainly have been defeated in battle, and for years a constant wariness and tension have existed between the two groups. Neither group trusts the other.

The Koran declares: "To those against whom war is made, permission is given [to defend themselves], because they are wronged and verily, Allah is Most Powerful to give them Victory—[they are] those who have been expelled from their homes in defiance of right—[for no cause] except that they say, 'Our Lord is Allah'" (22:39–40).

The Koran also permits fighting to defend the religion of Islam. "Fight in the cause of Allah against those who fight against you, but do not transgress limits. Lo! Allah loves not aggressors. . . . And fight them until persecution is no more, and religion is for Allah" (2:190).

The Arabs believe they have been persecuted by Israel. The Koran further advises, "If you fear treachery from any group, throw back [their treachery] to them, [so as to be] on equal terms" (8:58). The prophet Muhammad undertook a number of armed campaigns to remove treacherous people from power. He launched armed campaigns against several tribes, defeated them, and exiled them from the land.

According to the Koran, Allah further advises his followers to defend themselves through preemptive strikes: "Fighting is prescribed upon you, and you dislike it. But it may happen that you dislike a thing which is good for you, and it may happen that you love a thing which is bad for you. And Allah knows and you know not" (2:216). Muhammad said, "Strive [Jahidu] against the disbelievers with your hands and tongues" (Sahih Ibn Hibban #4708).

"And why should you not fight in the cause of Allah and of those who, being weak, are ill-treated [and oppressed]? Men, women, and children, whose cry is: 'Our Lord! Rescue us from this town, whose people are oppressors; and raise for us from You, one who will protect; and raise for us from You, one who will help'" (4:75).

Regardless of the stipulations of Islamic law, there are many Islamic radicals bent on the destruction of the Jewish people. The strategy of Islamic Jihad is as simple as it is satanic: "Kill so many Jews that they will eventually abandon Palestine."[16]

The late Imam Hasan al-Bana of the Islamic Resistance Movement, HAMAS, summed up their philosophy so well that it was included in their covenant: "Israel will exist and will continue to exist until Islam will obliterate it, just as it obliterated others before it."[17]

But Israel will not be defeated easily. Her people are saying, "God gave us a blood covenant to this land forever, and we're not going to give it up. Our forefathers marched into the gas chambers singing *Hatikvah* [the anthem which speaks of the hope within the heart of all Jews to be members of a free people in the land of Zion and Jerusalem], but we will not willingly be slaughtered again. We are going to defend ourselves to the death if we are encircled, and if this is another Masada, so be it. We're standing our ground until hell freezes over."

To the Muslims, Israel is as troublesome as a cornered copperhead. But mark this: if the Arabs do not eventually defeat Israel in combat, Muhammad lied, the Koran is in error, and Allah is not the true God. These are heretical ideas to the Muslim—absolutely unthinkable. The existence and survival of Israel flies in the face of Muslim theology. As long as Israel survives, their triumph-based theology cannot be affirmed. So, despite the peace treaties, the conflict is not done. Many Muslims will continue to fight Israel at every opportunity.

"Our objective is the destruction of Israel," Arafat once said. "There is to be no compromise and no moderation. No, we do not want peace. We want war and victory. Peace for us means the destruction of Israel and nothing else.[19] . . . We shall fight together as one Muslim nation under one flag. We are all zealots of the Muslim faith. We shall all stand together under the Muslim flag."[20]

Can a devoted follower of the Muslim faith change his mind? Apparently he did, for Arafat himself signed the West Bank Accord in the White House, then shook hands with Yitzhak Rabin as the world watched.

Muslims have also persecuted Christians with bloody fervor. In July 1995, the *Wall Street Journal* reported that "the rise of Islamic fundamentalism has effectively criminalized the practice of Christianity."[21] Under Islamic apostasy doctrines, writes Michael Horowitz, "Muslim converts to Christianity may be punished by death. Until recently, such doctrines were routinely ignored by Islamic governments, or interpreted liberally. But particularly in the case of Christian converts and evangelical Protestants, this is no longer true."[22]

Of course there are many Muslims who sincerely want peace, but the radical, extremist Muslims who think Yassir Arafat has compromised still intend to destroy Israel and Jerusalem. These are the people who believe that anyone who will not confess that Allah is God, that Muhammad is his prophet, and that the Koran is the perfect fulfillment of God's Word, should be put to death.

Israel's Present

Why did Yigal Amir kill Rabin? He did it because he is part of the two-faced Janus that is Israel. Janus was the Roman god of doors and gateways, of beginnings. Janus, for whom the month of January was named, was always pictured with two faces looking in opposite directions, one young and one old.

Israel is like Janus: one face belongs to religious Jews who believe the holy Scriptures are absolute truth, that Israel has a divine mandate to possess the land and to build in it. Yet part of the same body is the other face, the nonreligious Jews who believe political solutions only come through the peace process. Rabin was like Janus: to many he represented the hope that Israel would emerge from isolation, persecution, and bloodshed to find acceptance in the modern world community. To others, he embodied the threat that Israel would negotiate away the national identity they had gained by conquest, United Nations charter, and divine right.[23]

Leah Rabin, visiting New York with her husband's successor, Prime Minister Shimon Peres, told a huge gathering at Madison Square Garden that Israel should strive for unity. "We are undergoing a crisis. We need to change the climate of hatred and violence that brought about the assassination," she told the crowd exactly one month after her husband's death. "In his death he bequeathed to us peace; he bequeathed to us solidarity; he bequeathed Jewish unity."[24]

Peres echoed the sentiments of Rabin's widow. "Yitzhak Rabin never tried to please you," he told the crowd. "He tried to lead you. That was his obligation. We do recognize the right of the opposition to oppose us. We do recognize the right of the opposition to try to change the government. But we do expect the opposition, with us, to make our nation free and democratic, having many views and remaining together. We should also be united against violence, against murder, against curses. Let's argue, not hate."[25]

Although the cry for peace and unity is being proclaimed with new passion, it is not new. The last time I was in Israel I witnessed a demonstration unlike anything I have ever seen in the United States. A great throng of people, marching side by side, line after line, came down the street shouting, "Peace now! Peace now!" They made a thunderous noise; the walls of the building vibrated with the sound of their protest.

After seeing that, I began to think that perhaps we Americans don't know what true political activism is! Everybody in Israel is politically active and passionate about their beliefs. The generation that survived the Holocaust and came to Palestine was united because they faced a common enemy. In Israel's early years, during the wars of 1948 and 1967, it was "us against them," and Israel fought for its life and placed its destiny in Jewish hands. But now the children of those soldiers are adults, and they are saying, "Times are changing, what happened to you is past, and we want peace now. If land is the price for peace, so be it; just give peace a chance. If the Syrians want the Golan Heights, give them the Golan Heights."

And so Israel stands with a Janus face before the world: young people who want peace at any price resist older, more skeptical people. But, as any zoologist will tell you, a two-headed creature will not survive long; a house divided against itself cannot stand. Israel will unite and peace will prevail . . . when the country accepts the false man of peace who steps out onto the world's stage.

Israel's Future

Israel holds clear title to the land she possesses. She has never, for any reason, forfeited that title. God has told His people,

> My mercy I will keep for him forever, and My covenant shall stand firm with him. His seed also I will make to endure forever, and his throne as the days of heaven. If his sons forsake My law and do not walk in My judgments, if they break My statutes and do not keep My commandments, then I will punish their transgression with the rod, and their iniquity with stripes. Nevertheless My lovingkindness I will not utterly take from him, nor allow My faithfulness to fail. My covenant I will not break, nor alter the word that has gone out of My lips. (Ps. 89:28–34)

God told Abraham that the land would belong to his offspring forever; He reminded the psalmist that He will not violate His covenant or change His mind. God is not like men; His promises are secure and eternal. We can trust them, and we can trust the prophecies He gave to His prophets.

The prophet Ezekiel writes of a time when Israel will be a land of unwalled villages, a land of peaceful and unsuspecting people. An enemy army will look upon a land that is resettled ruins and populated by people gathered from the nations, rich in livestock and goods.

Someone else will look upon her, too . . . the Antichrist.

CHAPTER THREE

The Panorama of Prophecy

B efore we delve further into the rapidly-approaching end times, let me introduce or reacquaint you with some terms referring to events in the last days.

The *Rapture* is the literal, physical "snatching away" of those who have placed their faith in Jesus Christ. The Rapture could come at any moment, and it will occur without warning. Every single member of the corporate body of Christ, the genuine believers, will be taken alive to "meet him in the air" (1 Thess. 4:17). Those who have suffered physical death will be resurrected with incorruptible, supernatural bodies.

The *Antichrist,* whom we will later discuss at length, will be revealed shortly after the Rapture has occurred. He is the man who will establish a one-world government, a one-world religion, and a one-world economy. He is also known by other names, among them "the Beast," and "666."

The *Tribulation* is the seven-year period which follows the disappearance of the Church. The Bible says this time will be a literal hell on earth, replete with famine, natural disasters, epidemic sickness, war, and treachery.

At the close of the time of tribulation, life on earth as we know it will change dramatically. Israel's Messiah will come to earth as a reigning king to vanquish the enemy armies which have surrounded Israel. With him will come the heavenly armies, clothed in white. Satan and the Antichrist will be defeated, and Satan will be bound. The Messiah will establish an earthly kingdom of peace and righteousness which will last for one thousand years. People who have survived the Tribulation will sing, "Joy to the world, the Lord has come, let Earth receive her king!" This thousand-year reign of the Messiah is known as the *Millennium*.

Because God created man with a free will and wants man to freely choose to worship Him, after one thousand years Satan will be released. The Deceiver will be allowed to attempt to convince the people of the millennial world that he is worthy of worship. But once again God will step in with His heavenly armies and Satan's uprising will be defeated.

At that point, every person who has ever lived will stand before the throne of God at the event called the *Great White Throne Judgment*. There every man and woman, rich or poor, great or small, will be judged according to whether he or she accepted or rejected the King of Kings and Lord of Lords, Israel's Messiah, Jesus the Christ. Those who have accepted Him will enter into blessed eternity; those who have rejected Him will depart God's presence and join Satan in the eternal fires of hell. This present earth will be destroyed with a "great and fervent heat," and God will create a new heaven and a new earth in which we will dwell for eternity (see 2 Pet. 3:10–13).

Nebuchadnezzar's Dream

The second chapter of Daniel gives a glimpse of the end times. God sent Nebuchadnezzar, king of Babylon, a dream of an image that perfectly describes the empires that would rule the earth from the time of the Babylonian king until the end of the world.

A major obstacle facing those who tried to interpret Nebuchadnezzar's dream was the fact that he forgot it. He decreed that if his magicians, astrologers, and sorcerers could not reveal his dream and its meaning, they would be "cut into pieces" and their houses turned into "piles of rubble." Since the king's wise men had no choice but to produce or perish, the occult crowd began to massage their chicken bones and call upon their gods of darkness to reveal the king's forgotten dream.

No answers came. They went as a group before Nebuchadnezzar and said, "There is not a man on earth who can tell the king's matter; therefore no king, lord, or ruler has ever asked such things of any magician, astrologer, or Chaldean. It is a difficult thing that the king requests, and there is no other who can tell it to the king except the gods, whose dwelling is not with flesh" (vv. 10–11).

THE FOUR KINGDOMS

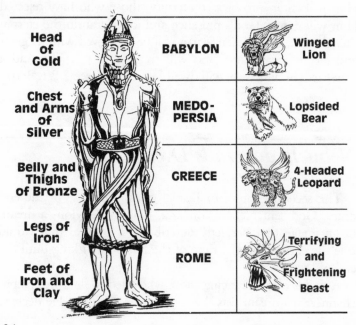

Head of Gold	BABYLON		Winged Lion
Chest and Arms of Silver	MEDO-PERSIA		Lopsided Bear
Belly and Thighs of Bronze	GREECE		4-Headed Leopard
Legs of Iron Feet of Iron and Clay	ROME		Terrifying and Frightening Beast

Enter Daniel, a Jewish captive from Jerusalem, who served the living God of Abraham, Isaac, and Jacob. The Bible tells us that "the secret was revealed to Daniel in a night vision. So Daniel blessed the God of heaven" (v. 19).

In the presence of the mortified astrologers, magicians, and sorcerers, Daniel went before King Nebuchadnezzar and proclaimed,

> But there is a God in heaven who reveals secrets, and He has made known to King Nebuchadnezzar what will be in the latter days. Your dream, and the visions of your head upon your bed, were these: As for you, O king, thoughts came to your mind while on your bed, about what would come to pass after this; and He who reveals secrets has made known to you what will be. But as for me, this secret has not been revealed to me because I have more wisdom than anyone living, but for our sakes who make known the interpretation to the king, and that you may know the thoughts of your heart. (vv. 28–30)

Can't you just see those astrologers squirming? They had just proclaimed that God would not bother to speak to lowly men, and yet Daniel had a direct hot line to heaven!

Daniel paid them no attention, but went on proclaiming the things which were to come:

> You, O king, were watching; and behold, a great image! This great image, whose splendor was excellent, stood before you; and its form was awesome. This image's head was of fine gold, its chest and arms of silver, its belly and thighs of bronze, its legs of iron, its feet partly of iron and partly of clay. You watched while a stone was cut out without hands, which struck the image on its feet of iron and clay, and broke them in pieces. Then the iron, the clay, the bronze, the silver, and the gold were crushed together, and became like chaff from the summer threshing floors; the wind carried them away so that no trace of them was found. And the stone that struck the image became a great mountain and filled the whole earth. This is the dream. (vv. 31–36)

I'm sure Nebuchadnezzar was about to rise up off his throne as Daniel's words touched the chords of memory in his mind. Yes, he remembered the image, and yes, he knew it spoke of something dreadfully important! But what did it all mean? He did not interrupt as Daniel continued to speak.

> Now we will tell the interpretation of it before the king. You, O king, are a king of kings. For the God of heaven has given you a kingdom, power, strength, and glory; and wherever the children of men dwell, or the beasts of the field and the birds of the heaven, He has given them into your hand, and has made you ruler over them all—you are this head of gold. But after you shall arise another kingdom inferior to yours; then another, a third kingdom of bronze, which shall rule over all the earth. And the fourth kingdom shall be as strong as iron, inasmuch as iron breaks in pieces and shatters everything; and like iron that crushes, that kingdom will break in pieces and crush all the others. Whereas you saw the feet and toes, partly of potter's clay and partly of iron, the kingdom shall be divided; yet the strength of the iron shall be in it, just as you saw the iron mixed with ceramic clay. And as the toes of the feet were partly of iron and partly of clay, so the kingdom shall be partly strong and partly fragile. As you saw iron mixed with ceramic clay, they will mingle with the seed of men; but they will not adhere to one another, just as iron does not mix with clay. And in the days of these kings the God of heaven will set up a kingdom which shall never be destroyed; and the kingdom shall not be left to other people; it shall break in pieces and consume all these kingdoms, and it shall stand forever. Inasmuch as you saw that the stone was cut out of the mountain without hands, and that it broke in pieces the iron, the bronze, the clay, the silver, and the gold—the great God has made known to the king what will come to pass after this. The dream is certain, and its interpretation is sure. (vv. 36–45)

History has proven Daniel's interpretation of Nebuchadnezzar's dream to be accurate. As Daniel prophesied, the empire which supplanted Nebuchadnezzar's head of gold was the

Medo-Persian, the breastplate of silver. The powerful Babylonians were displaced by Alexander the Great of Greece, the loins of brass. Alexander's empire fell to the Roman Empire, the strong and mighty domain which eventually divided into eastern and western empires.

You'll notice that as Daniel's eye traveled down the image, the strength of the metals progressed from soft (gold) to very hard (iron). This is a prophetic picture of the military strength of nations that would develop in years to come. Mankind has progressed from relatively weak weapons such as spears and cudgels to smart bombs, scud missiles, and thermonuclear devices that could leave Earth a spinning graveyard in space.

It is important to note that the strength of the iron kingdom seemed to be diluted over time. The lower the eye descends, the weaker the material becomes, until the feet are composed of iron and clay, two materials which simply will not blend with each other. The "partly strong and partly broken" kingdom of Rome did weaken as it aged, until it finally divided into ten toes, or ten kingdoms. Though several biblical commentators have made lists of the ten kingdoms, few writers agree as to which kingdoms or nations the ten toes actually represent. Prophecy scholar Dwight Pentecost says, "The ten kingdoms are to exist at one time, not through a period of several centuries, and all are to form one confederation. There is nothing in the past history of the kingdoms of Europe that answers to this."[1]

What are the two substances that will not mix? Scholar William Kelly suggests that the final form of power from the old Roman Empire will be a federation composed of autocracies and democracies, represented by iron and clay. In his view, iron represents nations ruled by a monarch; clay represents nations which adhere to a democratic or representative form of government.[2]

These ten toes, or empires, will be some sort of European federation. Today there are sixteen members of the European Union (formerly known as the European Common Market), fifteen members of the European Council, sixteen members of NATO, and thirty-three members of the Council of Europe. The Antichrist could spring from any of these groups. Just as the original six nations of the European Common Market grew to the sixteen member European Union, any of these groups could consolidate to ten.

The Bible revealed that a confederated union of ten nations will exist in the last days. These ten nations—some ruled by monarchs, some by democratic governments—could very well be the "ten toes" to be crushed by the stone cut without hands, Israel's Messiah. Nebuchadnezzar's image, representing the glorious and powerful kingdoms of the world, will be ground to powder and totally obliterated.

Daniel's Dream of Four Beasts

God wanted us to know the future, so He revealed to us the nations that would rule from Nebuchadnezzar through the terminal generation. Not only did he grant Nebuchadnezzar a vision of things to come, years later he repeated the same scenario with Daniel, this time using animals rather than metals. Why? Because animals have abilities and dispositions that vividly portray the profile and personality of coming kings and their kingdoms.

Listen to Daniel as he tells us about his dream in Daniel 7:

In the first year of Belshazzar king of Babylon, Daniel had a dream and visions of his head while on his bed. Then he wrote down the dream, telling the main facts.

Daniel spoke, saying, "I saw in my vision by night, and behold, the four winds of heaven were stirring up the Great Sea. And four great beasts came up from the sea, each different from the other. The first was like a lion, and had eagle's wings. I watched till its wings were plucked off; and it was lifted up from the earth and made to stand on two feet like a man, and a man's heart was given to it." (vv. 1–4)

In Daniel's dream we see the same parade of nations described in Nebuchadnezzar's vision, but with a different and disturbing twist.

During the reign of Belshazzar, Nebuchadnezzar's grandson, Daniel dreamed and saw four beasts rise up from the sea. The first beast was like a lion with the wings of an eagle: an exact representation of the Babylonian national symbol, a winged lion. Daniel had already seen the fulfillment of part of this vision. Nebuchadnezzar, who had risen to staggering heights of accomplishment, took pride in his success, but God struck him to the ground in a supernatural display of real power. Nebuchadnezzar lost his mind and actually ate grass like an ox for seven years, after which God restored his mind. He returned to his kingdom with "the heart of a man" and a new appreciation for the power of God.

But Babylon was doomed to failure. King Cyrus of Persia moved to capture the Babylonian empire in 539 B.C. and defeated Babylon's army on the Tigris River just south of modern-day Baghdad. The Babylonian Chronicle reports that the army of Cyrus entered Babylon without a battle.[3]

"And suddenly another beast, a second, like a bear. It was raised up on one side, and had three ribs in its mouth between its teeth. And they said thus to it: 'Arise, devour much flesh!'" (v. 5).

The second beast, a lopsided bear (because the Medes were more prominent than the Persians), represents the Medo-Persian Empire. The three ribs in the bear's mouth graphically illustrate the three prominent conquests of the empire: Lydia in 546 B.C., Babylon in 539 B.C., and Egypt in 525 B.C.[4]

"After this I looked, and there was another, like a leopard, which had on its back four wings of a bird. The beast also had four heads, and dominion was given to it" (v. 6).

The third beast, the leopard with four wings and four heads, represents Greece under Alexander the Great. The leopard is a swift animal, symbolizing the blinding speed with which Alexander's military juggernaut attacked its enemies.

What is the significance of the four heads? Through the telescope of history, their significance is clear. At age thirty-two, Alexander died in Babylon in 323 B.C. At his death, his four leading generals divided his kingdom: Ptolemy I took Israel and Egypt, Seleucus I reigned over Syria and Mesopotamia, Lysimachus chose to rule Thrace and Asia Minor, and Cassander took charge of Macedonia and Greece.

"After this I saw in the night visions, and behold, a fourth beast, dreadful and terrible, exceedingly strong. It had huge iron teeth; it was devouring, breaking in pieces, and trampling the residue with its feet. It was different from all the beasts that were before it, and it had ten horns" (v. 7).

The frightening fourth beast, more terrifying than its predecessors, represents the Roman Empire and the final form of Gentile power on the earth. The most important thing to notice about this horrifying beast is not its strength, its ferocity, or the fact that it has destroyed all the other beasts before it. The most important fact is that it has ten horns.

The ten horns of Daniel's dream correspond to the ten toes of Nebuchadnezzar's, and the horns represent ten kings or leaders who will lead nations that have risen from the fourth great world kingdom.

And while Daniel sat and thought about those ten leaders, another rose among them, a little one, who immediately uprooted or destroyed three of the ten. This horn had eyes like the eyes of a man and a mouth that spoke boastfully:

"I was considering the horns, and there was another horn, a little one, coming up among them, before whom three of the first horns were plucked out by the roots. And there, in this horn, were eyes like the eyes of a man, and a mouth speaking pompous words"(v. 8).

From among the ten kingdoms will arise one individual, the Antichrist, who will control the entire federation of nations.

Who is this "little horn"? And how can he wield enough power to control Europe, establish a worldwide religion, a worldwide economy, and a worldwide government? The answers to these questions can be found in God's Word, which we will discuss in coming chapters.

> I watched till thrones were put in place, and the Ancient of Days was seated; His garment was white as snow, and the hair of His head was like pure wool. His throne was a fiery flame, its wheels a burning fire; a fiery stream issued and came forth from before Him. A thousand thousands ministered to Him; ten thousand times ten thousand stood before Him. The court was seated, and the books were opened.
>
> I watched then because of the sound of the pompous words which the horn was speaking; I watched till the beast was slain, and its body destroyed and given to the burning flame. As for the rest of the beasts, they had their dominion taken away, yet their lives were prolonged for a season and a time.
>
> I was watching in the night visions, and behold, One like the Son of Man, coming with the clouds of heaven! He came to the Ancient of Days, and they brought Him near before Him. Then to Him was given dominion and glory and a kingdom, that all peoples, nations, and languages should serve Him. His dominion is an everlasting dominion, which shall not pass away, and His kingdom the one which shall not be destroyed. . . .
>
> This is the end of the account. As for me, Daniel, my thoughts greatly troubled me, and my countenance changed; but I kept the matter in my heart. (vv. 9–14, 28)

The Coming Victorious Messiah

Though Daniel's dream ended with the good news of the permanent reign of Christ, still he was troubled. Four great kingdoms would arise, and from them a ten-kingdom confederation. From the confederation would come a pompous destroyer who would finally be destroyed by the Son of Man. The victory would be God's, but not before the world had suffered greatly.

Notice that Daniel saw one like the Son of Man coming to God, the Ancient of Days. To Him was given the everlasting kingdom that would not be destroyed. Before Him all people of all nations bowed. They served and worshiped the Son of Man, who is the Son of God.

Just as present-day Israel has two faces, so does its Messiah. He is both a suffering servant and a reigning king. He is both a gentle shepherd and a victorious warrior.

God often allows us to see the future in the past. Consider the story of Joseph, the beloved son of Jacob. He was betrayed by vengeful, jealous brothers who planned his death but eventually sold him into slavery in Egypt. He suffered among people who were not of his heritage, and after many years of slavery and imprisonment, he was elevated to the second highest position in the land. His brothers, driven by the gnawing pain of hunger, ventured into Egypt and stood before Joseph three times before he revealed his identity.

The Jewish people, sons of Abraham, have now returned to their land three times. The first time was when they returned from Egypt under the direction of Moses. The second time they returned from captivity with Nehemiah to rebuild the wall. In 1948, they reclaimed their ancestral title to the land for the third time. Now, after this third visitation, they will recognize their Brother when He reveals Himself.

Joseph told the sons of Jacob, "I am your brother who you rejected, but I have been exalted" (see Gen. 45). Zechariah says,

> And I will pour on the house of David and on the inhabitants of Jerusalem the Spirit of grace and supplication; then they will look on Me whom they pierced. Yes, they will mourn for Him

as one mourns for his only son, and grieve for Him as one grieves for a firstborn. In that day there shall be a great mourning in Jerusalem, like the mourning at Hadad Rimmon in the plain of Megiddo. (Zech. 12:10–11)

The first time Messiah came He was a baby in a manger, surrounded by donkeys and goats. The next time He comes He will be mounted on a milk-white stallion thundering through the clouds of heaven with the armies of heaven following Him. On His head will be many crowns, for He will come back to this earth as King of kings and Lord of lords.

The first time He came He was brought before Pilate; He was dragged before Herod. He was mocked, spit upon, and forced to wear a scarlet robe of mockery. The next time He comes, Pilate shall be brought before Him. Herod will be dragged before Him. Hitler will be hauled before Him, and that infamous hater of the Jewish people will bow before the King of the Jews and confess that He is Lord to the glory of God the Father.

The first time He came He was nailed to a bitterly rugged cross where He suffered and bled and died alone. The next time He comes He will put His foot on the Mount of Olives and it shall split in half. He will walk across the Kidron Valley and through the eastern gate and set His throne up on the temple mount, and from there He shall reign for one thousand years in the Millennium. Following that will be the Great White Throne Judgment, after which time shall cease and eternity will begin.

In the words of Daniel, "To Him will be given dominion and glory and a kingdom. People of all nations and languages will serve Him. His dominion will be an everlasting dominion which shall not pass away. And His kingdom is the one which shall not be destroyed."

CHAPTER FOUR

Can You Trust Prophecy?

Yes, you may be thinking, some biblical predictions have come true, but Bible prophecy is so vague it could never affect the decisions or conclusions I will make about the future. Wrong!

The eternal and almighty God, creator of Heaven and Earth, reigns over the past, present, and the future. Henry Ward Beecher said, "The Bible is God's chart for you to steer by, to keep you from the bottom of the sea, and to show you where the harbor is, and how to reach it without running on rocks and bars."

God has given us His Word in prophecy because He has always wanted His people to understand His actions. When God decided to destroy Sodom and Gomorrah, He decided to warn Abraham: "Shall I hide from Abraham what I am doing?" He asked (Gen. 18:17).

And while giving Abraham title to the land of Israel, God placed him in a deep sleep and said,

> "Know certainly that your descendants will be strangers in a land that is not theirs, and will serve them, and they will afflict them four hundred years. And also the nation whom they serve I will judge; afterward they shall come out with great possessions. Now as for you, you shall go to your fathers in peace; you shall be buried at a good old age. But in the fourth generation they shall return here, for the iniquity of the Amorites is

not yet complete." . . . On the same day the LORD made a covenant with Abram, saying: "To your descendants I have given this land, from the river of Egypt to the great river, the River Euphrates." (Gen. 15:13–16, 18)

God displayed the entire panorama of future events concerning Abraham's descendants, and every word came to pass. Prophecy, even a relatively short-term prophecy like the one God gave Abraham, is important! I was at a gathering of evangelical pastors several years ago in Houston and a well-known preacher got up and said, "I do not study prophecy and I do not teach prophecy because I don't understand it and I don't think it's relevant for the twentieth century."

Friends, about one quarter of the Bible was prophetic when it was written! Why would God choose to make a quarter of His Word irrelevant or indecipherable? He didn't. He wants us to understand the things to come. Bible prophecy proves beyond any reasonable doubt that God knows and controls the future. He's not sitting on the circle of the earth as a mere observer, He is in charge!

Daniel Webster, writing in *Confession of Faith,* said, "I believe that the Bible is to be understood and received in the plain and obvious meaning of its passages; since I cannot persuade myself that a book intended for the instruction and conversion of the whole world, should cover its true meaning in such mystery and doubt, that none but critics and philosophers can discover it."[1]

If you doubt that the Word of God is accurate, consider the prophecies concerning a city called Tyre. In Ezekiel 26, God forecast the end of Tyre: many nations would come against it (Ezekiel. 26:3); Babylon would be the first to attack it (v. 7); Tyre's walls and towers would be broken down (vv. 4, 9); the stones, timbers, and debris of the city would be thrown into the sea (v. 12); its location would become a bare rock and a place for fishermen to dry their nets (vv. 4–5, 14); and the city of Tyre would never be rebuilt (v. 14).[2]

Tyre was no insignificant fishing village. It was a great city of Phoenicia and a prominent world capital for over two thousand years. Yet at the peak of its power, the prophet Ezekiel had the audacity to predict a violent future and ignominious end for the mighty city of Tyre. This downfall would come about because of the city's flagrant wickedness and arrogance, traits personified in its ruler, Ittobal II, who claimed to be God.[3]

History proved Ezekiel's words. Many nations did come against Tyre: first the Babylonians, then the Greeks, the Romans, the Muslims, and the Crusaders. After a thirteen-year siege, Nebuchadnezzar of Babylon broke down Tyre's walls and towers and massacred all of its inhabitants, except for those who escaped to an island fortress a half-mile out in the Mediterranean Sea. Centuries after Ezekiel had spoken, Alexander the Great conquered the island fortress of Tyre by building a causeway from Tyre's mainland to the island, using the millions of cubic feet of rubble left from the destroyed city. Thus Tyre was scraped bare as a kneecap, just as Ezekiel had predicted.[4]

And, astonishingly, Tyre has never been rebuilt. Despite its strategic and beautiful location, despite the fact that it contains the Springs of Reselain, which pump ten million gallons of fresh water daily, Tyre finally and irrevocably fell in A.D. 1291, never to be rebuilt. What covers those acres today? The drying nets of fishermen.[5]

In the last chapter of the book of Daniel there is an interesting prophecy: "Blessed is he who waits, and comes to the one thousand three hundred and thirty-five days" (Dan. 12:12).

What's the meaning of this verse? First, it's important to remember that prophecy often has both a primary literal fulfillment—in this case, of 1335 days, which will come to pass at the end of the age—and a secondary symbolic fulfillment, perhaps, in this case, years. (Consider Numbers 14:34: "According to the number of the days in which you spied out the land, forty days, God told the children of Israel, for each day you shall bear your guilt one year, namely forty years, and you shall know My rejection.") If it is possible for this verse to have a literal year-to-the-day fulfillment, then we have seen this verse come to pass in this century.

Let me explain. Islam began in A.D. 622. Shortly after this time, Jerusalem was taken by Muslims and occupied by them until A.D. 1917. In that year, Jerusalem was released by British General Edmund Henry Allenby, who rode into Jerusalem upon a white horse. About that time the British government proclaimed that the Jews would be permitted to return to their land. This proclamation, called the Balfour Amendment, was issued exactly thirteen hundred and thirty five years later according to the Islamic system of reckoning time. The coins of the Ottoman empire minted in that year bore the date "1335" on one side and "1917" on the other.

Daniel's prophecy may then mean that after 1335 years a time of blessedness would come to the land of Israel. Those who watched and waited would have the opportunity to enjoy great blessing. In 1917, many German Jews returned to Palestine. Many of those who passed up this opportunity remained in Germany and were unable to escape Hitler's genocide. Perhaps this is the blessing to which Daniel referred.

Messianic Prophecies

Recently a well-known preacher was on *Larry King Live*. King, who is Jewish, asked this nationally known pastor, "How do you know Jesus Christ was the Son of God?" The minister smiled and said, "I just have to accept that by faith."

Faith is important to God, for "without faith it is impossible to please Him" (Heb. 11:6), but our faith is not blind! Most of us find that the more we learn, the more our faith is assured by the facts. Many a seeker of God has begun to study the facts of Jesus' life and ministry and found Him more than worthy of complete and total faith. With a heart searching for truth, they have examined the facts, then proclaimed with heartfelt sincerity, "Jesus is Lord!"

God created our minds; He knows we are a people who want to understand. As a result, He has given us Bible prophecies that verify Jesus' claim to be the Messiah. Canon Liddon, a Bible scholar, says that there are 332 distinct predictions in the Old Testament which were literally fulfilled in Jesus Christ.[6] I have listed just eighty-eight of these which prove that Jesus Christ is the only man dead or alive who could possibly be the Messiah.

Many mainline Christian voices are now saying Jesus Christ is neither virgin-born nor the Messiah. Examine the evidence before you accept such a view.

My single purpose in writing this book is to prepare you for the future and the coming of the Antichrist. We have seen how accurate biblical prophecy is, and I can assure you that these events will come to pass. But just as the Antichrist is coming, you can be certain that the Messiah is also coming. Like the two faces of Janus which look forward and back, these two beings represent completely opposite spiritual kingdoms. One wants to destroy you, the Other wants to give you life. One will bathe the world in blood, the Other will bring the golden era of peace.

Let me introduce you to Jesus Christ, a Jewish Rabbi who came to Earth the first time as a suffering Savior and will come again as a conquering king and the Prince of Peace. His personality, advent, and agenda are clearly revealed through the following eighty-eight major prophecies related by the Old Testament prophets. The fulfillment of God's Word is as sure as night following day, and just as every prophecy about Jesus' first coming has been literally fulfilled, every prophecy relating to his second coming and the events of the end times will also come to pass exactly as God has predicted.

Moses Profiles the Messiah

God hinted at the coming Messiah as early as the Garden of Eden when He predicted the coming and mission of the Messiah: "And I will put enmity between you and the woman, and between your seed [the Serpent, Satan] and her Seed [the Messiah, Jesus Christ]; He shall bruise your head [Satan's destruction], And you shall bruise His heel [Messiah's death and Resurrection]" (Gen. 3:15). Then God again hints at the mission of the Messiah to Abraham:

> Now the LORD had said to Abram: "Get out of your country, from your family and from your father's house, to a land that I will show you. I will make you a great nation; I will bless you and make your name great; and you shall be a blessing. I will bless those who bless you, and I will curse him who curses you; *and in you all the families of the earth shall be blessed.*" (Gen. 12:1–3, emphasis mine)

But it was Moses who gave us the first extended biblical description of the coming Messiah. In Deuteronomy 18:18–19, Moses brings to Israel the following promise from God: "I will raise up for them a Prophet like you from among their brethren, and will put My words in His mouth, and He shall speak to them all that I command Him. And it shall be that whoever will not hear My words, which He speaks in My name, I will require it of him."

In Acts 3:22–26, the apostle Peter explains how this prophecy of Moses applies to Jesus Christ of Nazareth as Israel's Messiah:

> For Moses truly said to the fathers, "The LORD your God will raise up for you a Prophet like me from your brethren. Him you shall hear in all things, whatever He says to you. And it shall be that every soul who will not hear that Prophet shall be utterly destroyed from among the people." Yes, and all the prophets, from Samuel and those who follow, as many as have spoken, have also foretold these days. You are sons of the prophets, and

of the covenant which God made with our fathers, saying to Abraham, "And in your seed all the families of the earth shall be blessed." To you first, God, having raised up His Servant Jesus, sent Him to bless you, in turning away every one of you from your iniquities.

Moses' words established three facts: First, God promised to send to Israel a particular prophet at a later time. The language Moses uses is singular throughout: "*a* Prophet . . . *His* mouth . . . *He* shall speak." These words cannot describe the later prophets in Israel as a whole. They referred to one special Prophet.

Second, this Prophet would have unique authority, above all others who had gone before Him, and if anyone in Israel refused to hearken to this Prophet, God would bring judgment upon that person.

Third, this Prophet would be like Moses in ways that would distinguish Him from all other prophets. A careful comparison of lives of the two men reveals twenty-seven distinct parallels between the lives of Moses and Jesus.

1. **Both Moses and Jesus were born in a period when Israel was under foreign rule.**

   "Now there arose a new king over Egypt, who did not know Joseph. . . . Therefore they set taskmasters over them to afflict them with their burdens. And they built for Pharaoh supply cities, Pithom and Raamses" (Ex. 1:8, 11).

   "And it came to pass in those days that a decree went out from Caesar Augustus that all the world should be registered. This census first took place while Quirinius was governing Syria. So all went to be registered, everyone to his own city. Joseph also went up from Galilee, out of the city of Nazareth, into Judea, to the city of David, which is called Bethlehem, because he was of the house and lineage of David, to be registered with Mary, his betrothed wife, who was with child" (Luke 2:1–5).

2. **Cruel kings decided that both Moses and Jesus should be killed as infants.**

"Then the king of Egypt spoke to the Hebrew midwives, of whom the name of one was Shiphrah and the name of the other Puah; and he said, 'When you do the duties of a midwife for the Hebrew women, and see them on the birthstools, if it is a son, then you shall kill him; but if it is a daughter, then she shall live.' But the midwives feared God, and did not do as the king of Egypt commanded them, but saved the male children alive" (Ex. 1:15–17).

"Then Herod . . . was exceedingly angry; and he sent forth and put to death all the male children who were in Bethlehem and in all its districts, from two years old and under, according to the time which he had determined from the wise men" (Matt. 2:16).

3. **The faith of both Moses' and Jesus' parents saved their lives.**

"So the woman [the mother of Moses] conceived and bore a son. And when she saw that he was a beautiful child, she hid him three months. But when she could no longer hide him, she took an ark of bulrushes for him, daubed it with asphalt and pitch, put the child in it, and laid it in the reeds by the river's bank. And his sister stood afar off, to know what would be done to him" (Ex. 2:2–4).

"By faith Moses, when he was born, was hidden three months by his parents, because they saw he was a beautiful child; and they were not afraid of the king's command" (Heb. 11:23).

"Now when they had departed, behold, an angel of the Lord appeared to Joseph in a dream, saying, 'Arise, take the young Child [Jesus] and His mother, flee to Egypt, and stay there until I bring you word; for Herod will seek the young Child to destroy Him.' When he arose, he took the young Child and His mother by night and departed for Egypt" (Matt. 2:13–14).

4. **Both Moses and Jesus found protection for a time with the people of Egypt.**

   "And the child grew, and she brought him to Pharaoh's daughter, and he became her son. So she called his name Moses, saying, 'Because I drew him out of the water'" (Ex. 2:10).

   "When he arose, he took the young Child [Jesus] and His mother by night and departed for Egypt, and was there until the death of Herod, that it might be fulfilled which was spoken by the Lord through the prophet, saying, 'Out of Egypt I called My Son' (Matt. 2:14–15).

5. **Both Moses and Jesus displayed unusual wisdom and understanding.**

   "And Moses was learned in all the wisdom of the Egyptians, and was mighty in words and deeds" (Acts 7:22).

   "Now so it was that after three days they found Him [Jesus] in the temple, sitting in the midst of the teachers, both listening to them and asking them questions. And all who heard Him were astonished at His understanding and answers" (Luke 2:46–47).

6. **Both Moses' and Jesus' characters were marked by meekness and humility.**

   "Now the man Moses was very humble, more than all men who were on the face of the earth" (Num. 12:3).

   "[Jesus said,] 'Come to Me, all you who labor and are heavy laden, and I will give you rest. Take My yoke upon you and learn from Me, for I am gentle and lowly in heart, and you will find rest for your souls. For My yoke is easy and My burden is light'" (Matt. 11:28–30).

7. **Both Moses and Jesus were completely faithful to God.**

   "My servant Moses . . . is faithful in all My house" (Num. 12:7).

   "Therefore, holy brethren, partakers of the heavenly calling, consider the Apostle and High Priest of our confession, Christ Jesus, who was faithful to Him who appointed Him, as Moses also was faithful in all His house. For this One has been counted worthy of more glory than Moses, inasmuch as He who built the house has more honor than the house. For every house is built by someone, but He who built all things is God. And Moses indeed was faithful in all His house as a servant, for a testimony of those things which would be spoken afterward, but Christ as a Son over His own house, whose house we are if we hold fast the confidence and the rejoicing of the hope firm to the end" (Heb. 3:1–6).

8. **Both Moses and Jesus were rejected by Israel for a time.**

"And when [Moses] went out the second day, behold, two Hebrew men were fighting, and he said to the one who did the wrong, 'Why are you striking your companion?' Then he said [to Moses], 'Who made you a prince and a judge over us?'" (Ex. 2:13–14).

"Now when the people saw that Moses delayed coming down from the mountain, the people gathered together to Aaron, and said to him, 'Come, make us gods that shall go before us; for as for this Moses, the man who brought us up out of the land of Egypt, we do not know what has become of him'" (Ex. 32:1).

"The governor answered and said to them, 'Which of the two do you want me to release to you?' They said, 'Barabbas!' Pilate said to them, 'What then shall I do with Jesus who is called Christ?' They all said to him, 'Let Him be crucified!'" (Matt. 27:21–22).

9. **Both Moses and Jesus were criticized by their brothers and sisters.**

"Then Miriam and Aaron spoke against Moses because of the Ethiopian woman whom he had married; for he had married an Ethiopian woman" (Num. 12:1).

"For even His [Jesus'] brothers did not believe in Him" (John 7:5).

10. **Both Moses and Jesus were received by Gentiles after being rejected by Israel.**

"Moses fled [Egypt] and dwelt in the land of Midian. . . . Then Moses was content to live with the man [Reuel], and he gave Zipporah his daughter to Moses" (Ex. 2:15, 21).

"On the next Sabbath almost the whole city [Jerusalem] came together to hear the word of God. But when the Jews saw the multitudes, they were filled with envy; and contradicting and blaspheming, they opposed the things spoken by Paul. Then Paul and Barnabas grew bold and said, 'It was necessary that the word of God should be spoken to you first; but since you reject it, and judge yourselves unworthy of everlasting life, behold, we turn to the Gentiles. For so the Lord has commanded us: "I have set you as a light to the Gentiles, that you should be for salvation to the ends of the earth."' Now when the Gentiles heard this, they were glad and glorified the word of the Lord [Jesus]. And as many as had been appointed to eternal life believed" (Acts 13:44–48).

11. **Both Moses and Jesus prayed asking forgiveness for God's people.**

"Then Moses returned to the LORD and said, 'Oh, these people have committed a great sin, and have made for themselves a god of gold! Yet now, if You will forgive their sin—but if not, I pray, blot me out of Your book which You have written'" (Ex. 32:31–32).

"Then Jesus said [concerning those who were crucifying Him], 'Father, forgive them, for they do not know what they do'" (Luke 23:34).

12. **Both Moses and Jesus were willing to bear the punishment for God's people.**

"Then Moses returned to the LORD and said, 'Oh, these people have committed a great sin, and have made for themselves a god of gold! Yet now, if You will forgive their sin—but if not, I pray, blot me out of Your book which You have written'" (Ex. 32:31–32).

"For Christ also suffered once for sins, the just for the unjust, that He might bring us to God, being put to death in the flesh but made alive by the Spirit" (1 Pet. 3:18).

13. **Both Moses and Jesus endured a forty-day fast.**

"So he [Moses] was there with the LORD forty days and forty nights; he neither ate bread nor drank water. And He wrote on the tablets the words of the covenant, the Ten Commandments" (Ex. 34:28).

"And when He [Jesus] had fasted forty days and forty nights, afterward He was hungry" (Matt. 4:2).

14. **Both Moses and Jesus spoke with God face-to-face.**

"Not so with My servant Moses; He is faithful in all My house. I speak with him face to face, even plainly, and not in dark sayings; and he sees the form of the LORD" (Num. 12:7–8).

"But since then there has not arisen in Israel a prophet like Moses, whom the LORD knew face to face" (Deut. 34:10).

"No one has seen God at any time. The only begotten Son [Jesus], who is in the bosom of the Father, He has declared Him" (John 1:18).

15. **Both Moses and Jesus went up into a high mountain to have communion with God, taking some of their closest followers with them.**

"Then Moses went up [to Mount Sinai], also Aaron, Nadab, and Abihu, and seventy of the elders of Israel, and they saw the God of Israel. And there was under His feet as it were a paved work of sapphire stone, and it was like the very heavens in its clarity" (Ex. 24:9–10).

"Now after six days Jesus took Peter, James, and John his brother, led them up on a high mountain by themselves; . . . While he was still speaking, behold, a bright cloud overshadowed them; and suddenly a voice came out of the cloud, saying, 'This is My beloved Son, in whom I am well pleased. Hear Him!'" (Matt. 17:1, 5).

16. **After their mountaintop experiences, both Moses' and Jesus' faces shone with supernatural glory.**

"But whenever Moses went in before the LORD to speak with Him, he would take the veil off until he came out; and he would come out and speak to the children of Israel whatever he had been commanded. And whenever the children of Israel saw the face of Moses, that the skin of Moses' face shone, then Moses would put the veil on his face again, until he went in to speak with Him" (Ex. 34:34, 35).

"And He [Jesus] was transfigured before them. His face shone like the sun, and His clothes became as white as the light" (Matt. 17:2).

17. **God spoke audibly from heaven to both Moses and Jesus.**

"Moses spoke, and God answered him by voice. Then the LORD came down upon Mount Sinai, on the top of the mountain. And the LORD called Moses to the top of the mountain, and Moses went up" (Ex. 19:19–20).

"But Jesus answered them, saying, 'The hour has come that the Son of Man should be glorified. . . . Father, glorify Your name.' Then a voice came from heaven, saying, 'I have both glorified it and will glorify it again'" (John 12:23, 28).

18. **Both Moses' and Jesus' places of burial were attended by angels.**

"Yet Michael the archangel, in contending with the devil, when he disputed about the body of Moses, dared not bring against him a reviling accusation, but said, 'The Lord rebuke you!'" (Jude 9).

"And behold, there was a great earthquake; for an angel of the Lord descended from heaven, and came and rolled back the stone from the door, and sat on it. . . . But the angel answered and said to the women, 'Do not be afraid, for I know that you seek Jesus who was crucified. He is not here; for He is risen, as He said. Come, see the place where the Lord lay'" (Matt. 28:2, 5–6).

19. **Both Moses and Jesus appeared alive after their deaths.**

"And behold, Moses and Elijah appeared to them [Jesus, Peter, James, and John], talking with Him" (Matt. 17:3).

"Then, the same day at evening, being the first day of the week, when the doors were shut where the disciples were assembled, for fear of the Jews, Jesus [after his death, burial, and resurrection] came and stood in the midst, and said to them, 'Peace be with you.' When He had said this, He showed them His hands and His side. Then the disciples were glad when they saw the Lord" (John 20:19, 20).

20. **Both and Moses and Jesus were teachers.**

[Moses is speaking] "Now, O Israel, listen to the statutes and the judgments which I teach you to observe, that you may live, and go in and possess the land which the LORD God of your fathers is giving you" (Deut. 4:1).

"There was a man of the Pharisees named Nicodemus, a ruler of the Jews. This man came to Jesus by night and said to Him, 'Rabbi, we know that You are a teacher come from God; for no one can do these signs that You do unless God is with him'" (John 3:1–2).

21. **Both Moses and Jesus were shepherds to God's people.**

"You led Your people like a flock by the hand of Moses and Aaron" (Ps. 77:20).

"[Jesus said,] 'I am the good shepherd. The good shepherd gives His life for the sheep. . . . My sheep hear My voice, and I know them, and they follow Me'" (John 10:11, 27).

22. **Both Moses and Jesus revealed God's name to his people.**

"Then Moses said to God, 'Indeed, when I come to the children of Israel and say to them, "The God of your fathers has sent me to you," and they say to me, "What is His name?" what shall I say to them?' And God said to Moses, 'I AM WHO I AM.' And He said, 'Thus you shall say to the children of Israel, "I AM has sent me to you"'" (Ex. 3:13–14).

"[Jesus prayed:] 'I have manifested Your name to the men whom You have given Me out of the world. They were Yours, You gave them to Me, and they have kept Your word. . . . Now I am no longer in the world, but these are in the world, and I come to You. Holy Father, keep through Your name those whom You have given Me, that they may be one as We are. While I was with them in the world, I kept them in Your name'" (John 17:6, 11–12).

23. **Through both Moses and Jesus God gave His people food from a supernatural source.**

"When the dew was gone, thin flakes like frost on the ground appeared on the desert floor. When the Israelites saw it, they said to each other, 'What is it?' For they did not know what it was. Moses said to them, 'It is the bread the LORD has given you to eat'" (Ex. 16:14–15 NIV).

"And [Jesus] directed the people to sit down on the grass. Taking the five loaves and the two fish and looking up to heaven, he gave thanks and broke the loaves. Then he gave them to the disciples, and the disciples gave them to the people. They all ate and were satisfied, and the disciples picked up twelve basketfuls of broken pieces that were left over. The number of those who ate was about five thousand men, besides women and children" (Matt. 14:19–21 NIV).

24. **Both Moses and Jesus brought deliverance to God's people.**

"The LORD said [to Moses], 'I have indeed seen the misery of my people in Egypt. I have heard them crying out because of their slave drivers, and I am concerned about their suffering. So I have come down to rescue them from the hand of the Egyptians and to bring them up out of that land into a good and spacious land, a land flowing with milk and honey. . . . So now, go. I am sending you to Pharaoh to bring my people the Israelites out of Egypt'" (Ex. 3:7–8, 10 NIV).

"The scroll of the prophet Isaiah was handed to [Jesus]. Unrolling it, he found the place where it is written: 'The Spirit of the Lord is on me, because he has anointed me to preach good news to the poor. He has sent me to proclaim freedom for the prisoners and recovery of sight for the blind, to release the oppressed, to proclaim the year of the Lord's favor.' . . . And he began by saying to them, 'Today this scripture is fulfilled in your hearing'" (Luke 4:17–19, 21 NIV).

25. **Both Moses and Jesus brought healing to God's people.**

"The soul of the people [Israel] became very discouraged on the way. And the people spoke against God and against Moses. . . . So the LORD sent fiery serpents among the people, and they bit the people; and many of the people of Israel died. Therefore the people came to Moses, and said, 'We have sinned, for we have spoken against the LORD and against you; pray to the LORD that He take away the serpents from us.' So Moses prayed for the people. Then the LORD said to Moses, 'Make a fiery serpent, and set it on a pole; and it shall be that everyone who is bitten, when he looks at it, shall live.' So Moses made a bronze serpent, and put it on a pole; and so it was, if a serpent had bitten anyone, when he looked at the bronze serpent, he lived" (Num. 21:4, 6–9).

"Jesus went throughout Galilee, teaching in their synagogues, preaching the good news of the kingdom, and healing every disease and sickness among the people" (Matt. 4:23 NIV).

"He himself [Jesus] bore our sins in his body on the tree, so that we might die to sins and live for righteousness; by his wounds you have been healed" (1 Pet. 2:24 NIV).

26. **Both Moses and Jesus worked great miracles.**

"Since then, no prophet has risen in Israel like Moses, whom the LORD knew face to face, who did all those miraculous signs and wonders the LORD sent him to do in Egypt—to Pharaoh and to all his officials and to his whole land. For no one has ever shown the mighty power or performed the awesome deeds that Moses did in the sight of all Israel" (Deut. 34:10–12 NIV).

"Men of Israel, listen to this: Jesus of Nazareth was a man accredited by God to you by miracles, wonders and signs, which God did among you through him, as you yourselves know" (Acts 2:22 NIV).

27. **Both Moses and Jesus established and sealed with blood a covenant between God and His people.**

"Then [Moses] took the Book of the Covenant and read it to the people. They responded, 'We will do everything the LORD has said; we will obey.' Moses then took the blood, sprinkled it on the people and said, 'This is the blood of the covenant that the LORD has made with you in accordance with all these words'" (Ex. 24:7–8 NIV).

"When Christ came as high priest of the good things . . . He entered the Most Holy Place once for all by His own blood, having obtained eternal redemption. The blood of goats and bulls and the ashes of a heifer sprinkled on those who are ceremonially unclean sanctify them so that they are outwardly clean. How much more, then, will the blood of Christ, who through the eternal

Spirit offered himself unblemished to God, cleanse our consciences from acts that lead to death. . . . For this reason Christ is the mediator of a new covenant" (Hebrews 9:11–15).

Not only does Scripture paint a vivid picture of Christ's similarity to Moses the Deliverer, but the prophets foretold his coming and ministry for thousands of years. The prophets spoke both of a suffering Messiah and a kingly, conquering Messiah, and all these prophecies below were fulfilled by Jesus Christ at His first appearance.

1. **The Messiah will be born of a woman.**

    Prophecy: When Adam and Eve sinned in the Garden of Eden, God the Father made this statement to Satan: "And I will put enmity between you [Satan] and the woman, and between your offspring and hers; he will crush your head [destroy you], and you will strike his heel [hurt him]" (Gen. 3:15 NIV).

    Fulfillment: "But when the time had fully come, God sent his Son, born of woman, born under law" (Gal. 4:4 NIV).

    The Messiah's first coming was from a mother's womb, as is the case with everyone who is born. What is interesting in the passages above is that the woman is emphasized, not the man. This is because Jesus was conceived not through the joining of a man and woman but by the power of the Holy Spirit overshadowing the virgin Mary (see Luke 1:35).

2. **The Messiah will be born of a virgin.**

    Prophecy: "Therefore the Lord Himself will give you a sign: Behold, a virgin will be with child and bear a son, and she will call His name Immanuel" (Is. 7:14 NASB).

    Fulfillment: "Now in the sixth month the angel Gabriel was sent by God to a city of Galilee named Nazareth, to a virgin betrothed to a man whose name was Joseph, of

the house of David. The virgin's name was Mary. . . .
Then the angel said to her, 'Do not be afraid, Mary, for
you have found favor with God. And behold, you will
conceive in your womb and bring forth a Son, and shall
call His name JESUS.' . . . Then Mary said to the angel,
'How can this be, since I do not know a man [that is,
have not had sexual relations with a man]?' And the angel
answered and said to her, 'The Holy Spirit will come upon
you, and the power of the Highest will overshadow you;
therefore, also, that Holy One who is to be born will be
called the Son of God. . . . For with God nothing will be
impossible.' Then Mary said, 'Behold the maidservant of
the Lord! Let it be to me according to your word.' And
the angel departed from her" (Luke 1:26–27, 30–31, 34–
35, 37–38).

3. **The Messiah will be the Son of God.**

Prophecy: "I will surely tell of the decree of the LORD:
He said to Me, 'Thou art My Son, today I have begotten
Thee'" (Ps. 2:7 NASB).

Fulfillment: "And behold, a voice [God the Father's]
out of the heavens, saying, 'This is My beloved Son, in
whom I am well-pleased'" (Matt. 3:17 NASB).

"And the unclean spirits, whenever they saw Him, fell
down before Him and cried out, saying, 'You are the Son
of God'" (Mark 3:11).

Psalm 2:7 is a Royal Psalm, and in it the Messiah is
proclaiming the affirmation of the Father about the Son-
ship of the Messiah.

4. **The Messiah will be the Seed of Abraham.**

Prophecy: "In your [Abraham's] seed all the nations of
the earth shall be blessed, because you have obeyed My
voice" (Gen. 22:18).

"Abraham will surely become a great and powerful nation, and all nations on earth will be blessed through him"
(Gen. 12:3).

Fulfillment: "The book of the genealogy of Jesus Christ, the Son of David, the Son of Abraham" (Matt. 1:1).

"The promises were spoken to Abraham and to his seed. The Scripture does not say 'and to seeds,' meaning many people, but 'and to your seed,' meaning one person, who is Christ" (Gal. 3:16 NIV).

5. **The Messiah will be a Son of Isaac.**

Prophecy: "Then God said [to Abraham], 'Yes, but your wife Sarah will bear you a son, and you will call him Isaac. I will establish my covenant with him as an everlasting covenant for his descendants after him'" (Gen. 17:19 NIV).

Fulfillment: "Abraham was the father of Isaac, Isaac the father of Jacob, Jacob the father of Judah and his brothers . . . and Jacob the father of Joseph, the husband of Mary, of whom was born Jesus, who is called Christ" (Matt. 1:2, 16 NIV).

"Jesus, . . . the son of Isaac, . . ." (Luke 3:23, 34).

6. **The Messiah will be a son of Jacob.**

Prophecy: "I see him, but not now; I behold him, but not near; a star shall come forth from Jacob, and a scepter [ruler] shall rise from Israel, and shall crush through the forehead of Moab, and tear down all the sons of Sheth" (Num. 24:17 NASB).

Fulfillment: "Abraham was the father of Isaac, Isaac the father of Jacob, Jacob the father of Judah and his brothers . . . and Jacob the father of Joseph, the husband of Mary, of whom was born Jesus, who is called Christ" (Matt. 1:2, 16 NIV).

"Jesus, ... the son of Jacob, . . ." (Luke 3:23, 34).

7. **The Messiah will be from the tribe of Judah.**

Prophecy: "The scepter will not depart from Judah, nor the ruler's staff from between his feet, until he comes to whom it belongs and the obedience of the nations is his" (Gen. 49:10 NIV).

Fulfillment: "Judah begot Perez and Zerah by Tamar . . . and Jacob begot Joseph the husband of Mary, of whom was born Jesus who is called Christ" (Matt. 1:3, 16).

"Jesus, . . . the son of Judah, . . ." (Luke 3:23, 33).

"For it is evident that our Lord arose from Judah" (Heb. 7:14).

8. **The Messiah will be of the family line of Jesse.**

Prophecy: "Then a shoot will spring from the stem of Jesse, and a branch from his roots will bear fruit" (Is. 11:1 NASB).

Fulfillment: "And Jesse begot David the king . . . and Jacob begot Joseph the husband of Mary, of whom was born Jesus who is called Christ" (Matt. 1:6, 16).

"Jesus, . . . the son of Jesse, . . ." (Luke 3:23, 32).

The prophecy of Isaiah is figurative language, depicting Jesse as the stem of a tree, and the "shoot" which shall come as someone from his lineage. Isaiah predicted that one would come from Jesse's line and bear much fruit. Jesus Christ, who descended from the line of Jesse, has borne much spiritual fruit—more than anyone else in history. Those who trust Him as Savior are reborn in Him, becoming the children of God through the power of His name, and manifesting spiritual fruit through Him.

9. **The Messiah will be of the house of David.**

Prophecy: "For to us a child is born, to us a son is given, and the government will be on his shoulders. And he will be called Wonderful Counselor, Mighty God, Everlasting Father, Prince of Peace. Of the increase of his government and peace there will be no end. He will reign on David's throne and over his kingdom, establishing and upholding it with justice and righteousness from that time on and forever. The zeal of the LORD Almighty will accomplish this" (Is. 9:6–7 NIV).

Fulfillment: "David the king begot Solomon by her who had been the wife of Uriah . . . and Jacob begot Joseph the husband of Mary, of whom was born Jesus who is called Christ" (Matthew 1:6, 16).

"Jesus, . . . the son of David, . . ." (Luke 3:23, 31).

Jesus descended from the lineage of David, and in His future millennial kingdom He will uphold the world with righteousness and justice. One day He, as a son of David, will rule from the Temple Mount in Jerusalem, and His kingdom will last forever.

10. **The Messiah will be born at Bethlehem.**

Prophecy: "But as for you, Bethlehem Ephrathah, too little to be among the clans of Judah, from you One will go forth for Me to be ruler in Israel. His goings forth are from long ago, from the days of eternity" (Mic. 5:2 NASB).

Fulfillment: "Jesus was born in Bethlehem of Judea" (Matt. 2:1).

11. **A star will announce the birth of the Messiah.**

Prophecy: "I see him, but not now; I behold him, but not near; a star shall come forth from Jacob, and a scepter [ruler] shall rise from Israel, and shall crush through the forehead of Moab, and tear down all the sons of Sheth" (Num. 24:17 NASB).

Fulfillment: "Now after Jesus was born in Bethlehem of Judea in the days of Herod the king, behold, wise men from the East came to Jerusalem, saying, 'Where is He who has been born King of the Jews? For we have seen His star in the East and have come to worship Him'" (Matt. 2:1–2).

A Bible commentator notes, "Many feel the Magi's comments reflected a knowledge of Balaam's prophecy concerning the star that would come out of Jacob."[7]

12. **Herod will kill the children.**

Prophecy: "Thus says the LORD, 'A voice is heard in Ramah, lamentation and bitter weeping. Rachel is weeping for her children; she refuses to be comforted for her children, because they are no more'" (Jer. 31:15 NASB).

Fulfillment: "Then when Herod saw that he had been tricked by the magi, he became very enraged, and sent and slew all the male children who were in Bethlehem and in all its environs, from two years old and under, according to the time which he had ascertained from the magi" (Matt. 2:16 NASB).

Wise men came from the east and told Herod that a new king had been born, this one to rule the Jews. Politically, Herod could not afford another uprising in the lands he oversaw for Rome, and the title, King of the Jews, was at the moment his. So, not knowing the exact identity of the newborn King, he decreed that all babies two years old and younger should be slaughtered in the desperate hope that by doing so the infant King would be among those killed.

13. **The Messiah has preexisted.**

Prophecy: "But as for you, Bethlehem Ephrathah, too little to be among the clans of Judah, from you One will go forth for Me to be ruler in Israel. His goings forth are from long ago, from the days of eternity" (Mic. 5:2).

Fulfillment: "And He is [has existed prior to] before all things, and in Him all things consist" (Col. 1:17).

14. **The Messiah shall be called "Lord."**

Prophecy: "The LORD says to my Lord: 'Sit at My right hand, until I make Thine enemies a footstool for Thy feet'" (Ps. 110:1 NASB).

Fulfillment: "Then Jesus answered and said, while He taught in the temple, 'How is it that the scribes say that the Christ is the Son of David? For David himself said by the Holy Spirit: "The LORD said to my Lord, 'Sit at My right hand, till I make Your enemies Your footstool.'" Therefore David himself calls Him "Lord"; how is He then his Son?' And the common people heard Him gladly" (Mark 12:35–37).

The Bible Knowledge Commentary examines David's prophecy: "David heard a heavenly conversation between the Lord *(Yahweh)* and David's Lord *('adonay),* that is, between God the Father and the Messiah. The verb *says* is . . . a word often used to depict an oracle or a revelation. In this oracle Yahweh said that David's Lord, the Messiah, is seated at Yahweh's right hand (cf. v. 5), the place of authority, until the consummation of the ages (cf. 2:8–9). At that time the Lord will send David's Lord, [Jesus] the Messiah, to make His enemies subject to Him. A footstool pictures complete subjugation. With His scepter the Messiah will . . . rule over His enemies."[8]

15. **The Messiah shall be called Immanuel (God with us).**

Prophecy: "Therefore the Lord Himself will give you a sign: Behold, a virgin will be with child and bear a son, and she will call His name Immanuel" (Is. 7:14 NASB).

Fulfillment: "'Behold, the virgin shall be with child, and bear a Son, and they shall call His name Immanuel,' which is translated, 'God with us.' Then Joseph, being aroused from sleep, did as the angel of the Lord commanded him and took to him his wife, and did not know her till she had brought forth her firstborn Son. And he called His name Jesus" (Matt. 1:23–25).

16. **The Messiah shall be a prophet.**

Prophecy: "I will raise up a prophet from among their countrymen like you, and I will put My words in his mouth, and he shall speak to them all that I command him" (Deut. 18:18 NASB).

Fulfillment: "And the multitudes were saying, 'This is the prophet Jesus, from Nazareth in Galilee'" (Matt. 21:11 NASB).

17. **The Messiah shall be a priest.**

Prophecy: "The LORD has sworn and will not change His mind, 'Thou art a priest forever according to the order of Melchizedek'" (Ps. 110:4 NASB).

Fulfillment: "Therefore, holy brethren, partakers of a heavenly calling, consider Jesus, the Apostle and High Priest of our confession" (Heb. 3:1 NASB).

"During the days of Jesus' life on earth, he offered up prayers and petitions with loud cries and tears to the one who could save him from death, and he was heard because of his reverent submission. Although he was a son, he learned obedience from what he suffered and, once made perfect, he became the source of eternal salvation for all who obey him and was designated by God to be high priest in the order of Melchizedek" (Heb. 5:7–10 NIV).

18. **The Messiah shall be a judge.**

Prophecy: "For the LORD is our Judge, the LORD is our Lawgiver, the LORD is our King; He will save us" (Is. 33:22).

Fulfillment: "I charge you therefore before God and the Lord Jesus Christ, who will judge the living and the dead at His appearing and His kingdom" (2 Tim. 4:1).

God the Father has given the role of Judge to Jesus Christ. On one day still to come, every man, woman, and child will stand before Jesus Christ the judge and acknowledge that He is Lord.

19. **The Messiah shall be King.**

Prophecy: "Of the increase of his government and peace there will be no end. He will reign on David's throne and over his kingdom, establishing and upholding it with justice and righteousness from that time on and forever.

The zeal of the Lord Almighty will accomplish this" (Is. 9:7 NIV).

Fulfillment: "'You are a king, then!' said Pilate. Jesus answered, 'You are right in saying I am a king. In fact, for this reason I was born, and for this I came into the world, to testify to the truth. Everyone on the side of truth listens to me'" (John 18:37 NIV).

20. **The Messiah shall be anointed by the Holy Spirit.**

Prophecy: "And the Spirit of the LORD will rest on Him, the spirit of wisdom and understanding, the spirit of counsel and strength, the spirit of knowledge and the fear of the LORD" (Is. 11:2 NASB).

Fulfillment: "And after being baptized, Jesus went up immediately from the water; and behold, the heavens were opened, and he saw the Spirit of God descending as a dove, and coming upon Him, and behold, a voice out of the heavens, saying, 'This is My beloved Son, in whom I am well-pleased'" (Matt. 3:16–17 NASB).

21. **The Messiah will have great zeal for God.**

Prophecy: "Because zeal for Your house has eaten me up, and the reproaches of those who reproach You have fallen on me" (Ps. 69:9).

Fulfillment: "Now the Passover of the Jews was at hand, and Jesus went up to Jerusalem. And He found in the temple those who sold oxen and sheep and doves, and the moneychangers doing business. When He had made a whip of cords, He drove them all out of the temple, with the sheep and the oxen, and poured out the changers' money and overturned the tables. And He said to those who sold doves, 'Take these things away! Do not make My Father's house a house of merchandise!' Then His disciples remembered that it was written, 'Zeal for Your house has eaten Me up'" (John 2:13–17).

22. The Messiah will be preceded by a messenger.

Prophecy: "A voice is calling, 'Clear the way for the LORD in the wilderness; make smooth in the desert a highway for our God'" (Is. 40:3 NASB).

Fulfillment: "In those days John the Baptist came preaching in the wilderness of Judea, and saying, 'Repent, for the kingdom of heaven is at hand!' For this is he who was spoken of by the prophet Isaiah, saying: 'The voice of one crying in the wilderness: "Prepare the way of the LORD; make His paths straight"'" (Matt. 3:1–3).

23. The Messiah will minister in Galilee.

Prophecy: "But there will be no more gloom for her who was in anguish; in earlier times He treated the land of Zebulun and the land of Naphtali with contempt, but later on He shall make it glorious, by the way of the sea, on the other side of Jordan, Galilee of the Gentiles" (Is. 9:1 NASB).

Fulfillment: "Now when Jesus heard that John had been put in prison, He departed to Galilee. And leaving Nazareth, He came and dwelt in Capernaum, which is by the sea, in the regions of Zebulun and Naphtali, that it might be fulfilled which was spoken by Isaiah the prophet, saying: 'The land of Zebulun and the land of Naphtali, by the way of the sea, beyond the Jordan, Galilee of the Gentiles: The people who sat in darkness have seen a great light, and upon those who sat in the region and shadow of death light has dawned.' From that time Jesus began to preach and to say, 'Repent, for the kingdom of heaven is at hand'" (Matt. 4:12–17).

The prophecy of Isaiah was "fulfilled when Jesus ministered in Capernaum— near the major highway from Egypt to Damascus, called 'the way of the sea.'"[9]

24. The Messiah's ministry will include miracles.

Prophecy: "Then the eyes of the blind will be opened, and the ears of the deaf will be unstopped. Then the lame will leap like a deer, and the tongue of the dumb will shout for joy" (Is. 35:5–6 NASB).

Fulfillment: "And Jesus was going about all the cities and the villages, teaching in their synagogues, and proclaiming the gospel of the kingdom, and healing every kind of disease and every kind of sickness" (Matt. 9:35 NASB).

25. The Messiah will be a teacher of parables.

Prophecy: "I [the prophet is speaking for the Messiah] will open my mouth in a parable; I will utter dark sayings of old" (Ps. 78:2).

"And He said, 'Go, and tell this people: "Keep on hearing, but do not understand; keep on seeing, but do not perceive." Make the heart of this people dull, and their ears heavy, and shut their eyes; lest they see with their eyes, and hear with their ears, and understand with their heart, and return and be healed'" (Is. 6:9–10).

Fulfillment: "All these things Jesus spoke to the multitude in parables; and without a parable He did not speak to them, that it might be fulfilled which was spoken by the prophet, saying: 'I will open My mouth in parables; I will utter things kept secret from the foundation of the world'" (Matt. 13:34–35).

"Then His disciples asked Him, saying, 'What does this parable mean?' And He said, 'To you it has been given to know the mysteries of the kingdom of God, but to the rest it is given in parables, that "Seeing they may not see, and hearing they may not understand"'" (Luke 8:9–10).

26. The Messiah will enter the temple.

Prophecy: "And the Lord, whom you seek, will suddenly come to His temple" (Mal. 3:1).

Fulfillment: "Then Jesus went out and departed from the temple, and His disciples came up to show Him the buildings of the temple. And Jesus said to them, 'Do you not see all these things? Assuredly, I say to you, not one stone shall be left here upon another, that shall not be thrown down'" (Matt. 24:1–2).

All Jews of Jesus' day entered the outer courts of the Temple, but this prophecy clearly indicates that Messiah would come when the Temple existed. The Temple at Jerusalem was destroyed in A.D. 70, so no would-be Messiah has been able to fulfill this prophecy since that date.

27. **The Messiah would enter Jerusalem on a donkey.**

Prophecy: "Rejoice greatly, O daughter of Zion! Shout in triumph, O daughter of Jerusalem! Behold, your king is coming to you; He is just and endowed with salvation, humble, and mounted on a donkey, even on a colt, the foal of a donkey" (Zech. 9:9 NASB).

Fulfillment: "Now when they drew near Jerusalem, and came to Bethphage, at the Mount of Olives, then Jesus sent two disciples, saying to them, 'Go into the village opposite you, and immediately you will find a donkey tied, and a colt with her. Loose them and bring them to Me. And if anyone says anything to you, you shall say, "The Lord has need of them," and immediately he will send them.' All this was done that it might be fulfilled which was spoken by the prophet, saying: 'Tell the daughter of Zion, "Behold, your King is coming to you, lowly, and sitting on a donkey, a colt, the foal of a donkey."'' So the disciples went and did as Jesus commanded them. They brought the donkey and the colt, laid their clothes on them, and set Him on them" (Matt. 21:1–7).

28. **The Messiah will be a "stone of stumbling" to the Jews.**

Prophecy: "The stone which the builders rejected Has become the chief cornerstone" (Ps. 118:22).

Fulfillment: "Therefore it is also contained in the Scripture, 'Behold, I lay in Zion a chief cornerstone, elect, precious, and he who believes on Him [Jesus] will by no means be put to shame.' Therefore, to you who believe,

He is precious; but to those who are disobedient, 'The stone which the builders rejected Has become the chief cornerstone,' and 'A stone of stumbling and a rock of offense'" (1 Pet. 2:6–8).

29. **The Messiah will be a light to the Gentiles.**

Prophecy: "I, the LORD, have called You in righteousness, and will hold Your hand; I will keep You and give You as a covenant to the people, as a light to the Gentiles, to open blind eyes, to bring out prisoners from the prison, those who sit in darkness from the prison house" (Is. 42:6–7).

Fulfillment: "The people who sat in darkness have seen a great light, and upon those who sat in the region and shadow of death light has dawned" (Matt. 4:16).

"A light [Jesus, the Messiah] to bring revelation to the Gentiles, and the glory of Your people Israel" (Luke 2:32).

The following prophecies from the Old Testament (numbers 30 through 58), were spoken by many different voices over a period of five hundred years, yet all of them were fulfilled in Jesus Christ during a single twenty-four hour period.

30. **The Messiah will be betrayed by a friend.**

Prophecy: "Even my close friend, in whom I trusted, who ate my bread, has lifted up his heel against me" (Ps. 41:9 NASB).

Fulfillment: "I [Jesus] do not speak concerning all of you. I know whom I have chosen; but that the Scripture may be fulfilled, 'He who eats bread with Me has lifted up his heel against Me.' Now I tell you before it comes, that when it does come to pass, you may believe that I am He. . . . Most assuredly, I say to you, one of you will betray Me" (John 13:18–19, 21).

"Judas Iscariot, who also betrayed Him" (Matt. 10:4).

Judas Iscariot, one of the trusted twelve disciples, ate the Passover dinner with Jesus the same night he betrayed Christ.

31. **The Messiah will be betrayed for thirty pieces of silver.**

    Prophecy: "And I said to them, 'If it is good in your sight, give me my wages; but if not, never mind!' So they weighed out thirty shekels of silver as my wages" (Zech. 11:12 NASB).

    Fulfillment: "Then one of the twelve, called Judas Iscariot, went to the chief priests and said, 'What are you willing to give me if I deliver Him [Jesus] to you?' And they counted out to him thirty pieces of silver. So from that time he sought opportunity to betray Him" (Matt. 26:14–16).

On the evening of the Passover dinner, Judas Iscariot, one of Jesus' twelve disciples, went to the chief priests and inquired if he might betray Jesus into their hands. As payment for his services, he was given thirty pieces of silver.

32. **The Messiah's "blood money" will be cast into God's house.**

    Prophecy: "So I took the thirty shekels of silver and threw them to the potter in the house of the LORD" (Zech. 11:13 NASB).

    Fulfillment: "And he [Judas] threw the pieces of silver into the sanctuary and departed (Matt. 27:5).

After betraying Jesus, Judas, overcome by remorse, threw the money back into the Temple and went outside and hanged himself.

33. **The price of betraying the Messiah will be given for a potter's field.**

    Prophecy: "So I took the thirty shekels of silver and threw them to the potter in the house of the LORD" (Zech. 11:13 NASB).

    Fulfillment: "And they [the chief priests and elders] counseled together and with the money [that had been thrown into the temple by Judas] bought the Potter's Field as a burial place for strangers" (Matt. 27:7 NASB).

The priests of the Temple, after hearing of Judas' end, decided to use the money to buy a field, where strangers were buried. It was known as the "potter's field."

34. The Messiah will be forsaken by his followers.

Prophecy: "Strike the Shepherd, and the sheep will be scattered" (Zech. 13:7).

Fulfillment: "Then Jesus said to them, 'All of you will be made to stumble because of Me this night, for it is written: "I will strike the Shepherd, and the sheep will be scattered."' . . . And they all forsook Him and fled" (Mark 14:27, 50).

The twelve disciples, who had followed Jesus faithfully for three years, fled into the night.

35. The Messiah will be accused by false witnesses.

Prophecy: "Malicious witnesses rise up; they ask me of things that I do not know" (Ps. 35:11 NASB).

Fulfillment: "Now the chief priests and the whole Council kept trying to obtain false testimony against Jesus, in order that they might put Him to death; and they did not find any, even though many false witnesses came forward" (Matt. 26:59–60 NASB).

The chief priests, trying to find fault with Jesus, bribed false witnesses to accuse Him of things He had no personal experience with—things He did not "know." Though, of course, He knew everything they would say and do.

36. The Messiah will be silent before his accusers.

Prophecy: "He was oppressed and He was afflicted, yet He did not open His mouth" (Is. 53:7 NASB).

Fulfillment: "And while He was being accused by the chief priests and elders, He answered nothing" (Matt. 27:12).

Throughout the litany of lies and false accusations, Jesus remained silent.

37. **The Messiah will be scourged and wounded.**

Prophecy: "But He was pierced through for our trans-gressions, He was crushed for our iniquities; the chasten-ing for our well-being fell upon Him, and by His scourging we are healed" (Is. 53:5 NASB).

Fulfillment: "Then he released Barabbas to them; and when he had scourged Jesus, he delivered Him to be cruci-fied" (Matt. 27:26).

38. **The Messiah will be smitten and spit upon.**

Prophecy: "I gave My back to those who struck Me, and My cheeks to those who plucked out the beard; I did not cover My face from shame and spitting" (Is. 50:6).

Fulfillment: "Then they spat in His face and beat Him with their fists; and others slapped Him" (Matt. 26:67 NASB).

39. **The Messiah will be mocked.**

Prophecy: "All those who see Me ridicule Me; they shoot out the lip, they shake the head, saying, 'He trusted in the LORD, let Him rescue Him; let Him deliver Him, since He delights in Him!'" (Ps. 22:7–8).

Fulfillment: "Then two robbers were crucified with Him, one on the right and another on the left. And those who passed by blasphemed Him, wagging their heads and saying, 'You who destroy the temple and build it in three days, save Yourself! If You are the Son of God, come down from the cross.' Likewise the chief priests also, mocking with the scribes and elders, said, 'He saved others; Himself He cannot save. If He is the King of Israel, let Him now come down from the cross, and we will believe Him. He trusted in God; let Him deliver Him now if He will have Him; for He said, "I am the Son of God."' Even the robbers who were crucified with Him reviled Him with the same thing" (Matt. 27:38–44).

40. **The Messiah will be weak; he will be an object of scorn.**
    Prophecy: "My knees are weak from fasting; and my flesh has grown lean, without fatness. I also have become a reproach to them; when they see me, they wag their head" (Ps. 109:24–25 NASB).

    Fulfillment: "And those who passed by blasphemed Him, wagging their heads and saying, 'Aha! You who destroy the temple and build it in three days, save Yourself, and come down from the cross!'" (Mark 15:29–30).

After a time without food, a beating, and intense interrogation, Jesus went out, carrying his cross, before a crowd of mocking, scornful onlookers.

41. **The Messiah's hands and feet will be pierced.**
    Prophecy: "They pierced My hands and My feet (Ps. 22:16).

    Fulfillment: "And when they came to the place called The Skull, there they crucified Him" (Luke 23:33 NASB).

It is interesting to note that this prediction of pierced hands and feet was made long before crucifixion was invented as a form of capital punishment. The psalmist wrote this prophecy over a thousand years before crucifixion was made common by the Romans, and the Jews never practiced crucifixion.

42. **The Messiah will be put to death alongside transgressors.**
    Prophecy: "Because He poured out Himself to death, and was numbered with the transgressors" (Is. 53:12 NASB).

    Fulfillment: "At that time two robbers were crucified with Him, one on the right and one on the left" (Matt. 27:38 NASB).

43. **The Messiah will intercede for his persecutors.**
    Prophecy: "Yet He Himself bore the sin of many, and interceded for the transgressors" (Is. 53:12 NASB).

Fulfillment: "Father, forgive them [those who were crucifying them]; for they do not know what they are doing" (Luke 23:34 NASB).

44. The Messiah will be rejected by his own people.

Prophecy: "He was despised and forsaken of men, a man of sorrows, and acquainted with grief; and like one from whom men hide their face, He was despised, and we did not esteem him" (Is. 53:3 NASB).

Fulfillment: "Then Pilate, when he had called together the chief priests, the rulers, and the people, said to them, 'You have brought this Man to me, as one who misleads the people. And indeed, having examined Him in your presence, I have found no fault in this Man concerning those things of which you accuse Him; no, neither did Herod, for I sent you back to him; and indeed nothing deserving of death has been done by Him. I will therefore chastise Him and release Him' (for it was necessary for him to release one to them at the feast). And they all cried out at once, saying, 'Away with this Man, and release to us Barabbas. . . . Crucify Him [Jesus], crucify Him!' Then he said to them the third time, 'Why, what evil has He done? I have found no reason for death in Him. I will therefore chastise Him and let Him go.' But they were insistent, demanding with loud voices that He be crucified. And the voices of these men and of the chief priests prevailed. So Pilate gave sentence that it should be as they requested. And he released to them the one they requested, who for rebellion and murder had been thrown into prison; but he delivered Jesus to their will" (Luke 23:13–18, 21–25).

45. The Messiah will be hated without a cause.

Prophecy: "Those who hate me without a cause are more than the hairs of my head" (Ps. 69:4).

Fulfillment: "But this happened that the word might be fulfilled which is written in their law, 'They hated Me without a cause'" (John 15:25).

Even though Jesus had done nothing wrong, the crowd clamored for His death, and He was hated.

46. **The Messiah's friends will stand afar off.**

Prophecy: "My loved ones and my friends stand aloof from my plague, and my relatives stand afar off" (Ps. 38:11).

Fulfillment: "And all his acquaintances and the women who accompanied Him from Galilee, were standing at a distance [from the events of Jesus' death], seeing these things" (Luke 23:49 NASB).

47. **People will shake their heads at the Messiah.**

Prophecy: "I also have become a reproach to them; when they see me, they wag their head" (Ps. 109:25 NASB).

Fulfillment: "And those who were passing by were hurling abuse at Him, wagging their heads" (Matt. 27:39 NASB).

48. **People will stare at the Messiah.**

Prophecy: "They look, they stare at me" (Ps. 22:17 NASB).

Fulfillment: "And the people stood looking on" (Luke 23:35).

49. **The Messiah's garments will be parted and lots cast for them.**

Prophecy: "They divided My garments among them, and for My clothing they cast lots" (Ps. 22:18).

Fulfillment: "Then the soldiers, when they had crucified Jesus, took His garments and made four parts, to each soldier a part, and also the tunic. Now the tunic was without seam, woven from the top in one piece. They said therefore among themselves, 'Let us not tear it, but cast lots for it, whose it shall be,' that the Scripture might be fulfilled which says: 'They divided My garments among them, and for My clothing they cast lots.' Therefore the soldiers did these things" (John 19:23–24).

Which did they do, divide the garments or cast lots? This statement seems almost contradictory until you realize what happened at the cross. They ripped the outer garment, but paused when they picked up the tunic. It was a fine piece of work, all in one piece, and so they decided to cast lots for it.

50. The Messiah will suffer thirst.

Prophecy: "And for my thirst they gave me vinegar to drink" (Ps. 69:21).

Fulfillment: "After this, Jesus . . . said, 'I thirst!'" (John 19:28).

51. They will offer the Messiah gall and vinegar to drink.

Prophecy: "They also gave me gall for my food, and for my thirst they gave me vinegar to drink" (Ps. 69:21).

Fulfillment: "They gave Him sour wine mingled with gall to drink. But when He had tasted it, He would not drink" (Matt. 27:34).

Gall is a poisonous, bitter herb. A stupefying drink, made of wine mingled with gall, was offered to Jesus, but he would not drink it.

52. The Messiah will utter a forsaken cry.

Prophecy: "My God, my God, why hast Thou forsaken me?" (Ps. 22:1 NASB).

Fulfillment: "And about the ninth hour Jesus cried out with a loud voice, saying, 'Eli, Eli Lama Sabachthani' that is, 'My God, My God, why hast Thou forsaken Me?'" (Matt. 27:46 NASB).

53. **The Messiah will commit himself to God.**

Prophecy: "Into Thy hand I commit my spirit" (Ps. 31:5 NASB).

Fulfillment: "And Jesus, crying out with a loud voice, said, 'Father, into Thy hands I commit My spirit!'" (Luke 23:46 NASB).

54. **None of the Messiah's bones will be broken.**

Prophecy: "He guards all his bones; not one of them is broken" (Ps. 34:20).

"And all My bones are out of joint" (Ps. 22:14).

Fulfillment: "But coming to Jesus, when they saw that He was already dead, they did not break His legs" (John 19:33 NASB).

While hanging on the cross by the hands and feet, it is very likely that all a man's bones would separate from their joints. The Romans used to hasten death by breaking the legs of the crucified criminals, but when they reached Jesus, they saw that He was already dead.

55. **The Messiah's heart will literally break.**

Prophecy: "My heart is like wax; it has melted within me" (Ps. 22:14).

Fulfillment: "But one of the soldiers pierced His side with a spear, and immediately blood and water came out" (John 19:34).

The blood and water which came forth from his side is believed by some to be evidence that Jesus' heart had literally burst. The appearance of both blood and water indicate that he had been dead long enough for the blood to separate into its component elements.

56. **The Messiah's side will be pierced.**

Prophecy: "They will look on Me whom they pierced" (Zech. 12:10).

Fulfillment: "But one of the soldiers pierced His side with a spear" (John 19:34).

57. Darkness will cover the land from noon until three o'clock.

Prophecy: "'And it will come about in that day,' declares the Lord God, 'that I shall make the sun go down at noon and make the earth dark in broad daylight'" (Amos 8:9 NASB).

Fulfillment: "Now from the sixth hour [noon] darkness fell upon all the land until the ninth hour [three o'clock]" (Matt. 27:45 NASB).

58. The Messiah will be buried in a rich man's tomb.

Prophecy: "His grave was assigned with wicked men, yet He was with a rich man in His death" (Is. 53:9 NASB).

Fulfillment: "There came a rich man from Arimathea, named Joseph . . . and asked for the body of Jesus. . . . When Joseph had taken the body, he wrapped it in a clean linen cloth, and laid it in his new tomb" (Matt. 27:57–60).

In fulfilling these last three prophecies, Jesus reflects the supernatural of the Messiah.

59. The Messiah would rise from the dead.

Prophecy: "For Thou wilt not abandon my soul to Sheol; neither wilt Thou allow Thy Holy One to undergo decay" (Psalm 16:10).

Fulfillment: "You seek Jesus of Nazareth, who was crucified. He is risen!" (Mark 16:6).

60. The Messiah will ascend to heaven.

Prophecy: "Thou hast ascended on high" (Ps. 68:18 NASB).

Fulfillment: "He [Jesus] was lifted up while they were looking on, and a cloud received Him out of their sight" (Acts 1:9 NASB).

61. **The Messiah will be seated at the right hand of God.**

Prophecy: "The LORD says to my Lord: 'Sit at My right hand, until I make Thine enemies a footstool for thy feet'" (Ps. 110:1 NASB).

Fulfillment: "When He had made purification of sins, He sat down at the right hand of the Majesty on high" (Heb. 1:3 NASB).

The prophecies listed above could not have been purposely fulfilled by Jesus Christ unless he was God. How could a mere man control the place or time of his birth? Why would a self-serving false messiah want to fulfill the manner of Christ's death and burial?

Some skeptics claim that sheer coincidence accounts for these fulfilled prophecies. You might be able to find some men whose lives would agree with a few of the above prophecies, but Jesus Christ is the only person, living or dead, who could have fulfilled all eighty-eight! And these are only a handful of the Messianic predictions found in Scripture.

I've included this section on Messianic prophecy to illustrate one key point: just as every prophecy about Jesus' first coming has been literally fulfilled, every prophecy relating to his second coming and the events of the end times will also be fulfilled . . . exactly as God has predicted.

We have seen how Jesus fulfilled Scripture related to His first coming as a suffering servant—prepare yourself for what the Bible predicts about His second coming at the conclusion of the last generation!

CHAPTER FIVE

Are We the Terminal Generation?

About two years ago, *Time* magazine's cover read, "Thinking the unthinkable!" The story stated that mankind is at the brink of disaster in a world bristling with nuclear weapons. Harvard professor Bernard Lown lamented that mankind is doomed, locked into a race toward Armageddon.

In December 1995, keepers of the famous Doomsday Clock moved the hands three minutes closer to midnight. Leonard Rieser, chairman of the Bulletin of the Atomic Scientists, reset the clock at fourteen minutes before midnight, or "Doomsday." As they announced the move, Rieser and his associates told the press that contrary to popular belief, the threat of nuclear apocalypse did not end with the Cold War.[1]

When Scripture tells us that heaven and earth will pass away, you can be sure that this world will definitely end. There will be a last baby born, a last marriage performed, a last kiss, a last song, a last hurrah. This world will not continue forever. The Second Law of Thermodynamics, otherwise known as the Law of Entropy, declares that all organized systems tend to disorder after time. Like all things, the earth, along with this physical universe, will wear out.

Ten Road Signs Confirming the End of the Age

When will the world end? And how? The Scriptures are not silent; God tells us when, how, and where the world as we know it will end: Armageddon.

Armageddon is the Hebrew word meaning "the mountain of Mageddo." The mountain of Mageddo lies east of Mount Carmel in the northern part of Israel. I've stood upon this mountain, and from its vantage point I could see a great extended plain stretching from the Mediterranean Sea eastward across the northern part of Israel.

Napoleon looked at the expanse of Armageddon and described it as the most natural battlefield on the face of the earth, for armies would be able to maneuver easily over its empty plains. On those plains, the Bible tells us, human blood will flow to the height of a horse's bridle for two hundred miles. There the false man of peace, the Antichrist, will join with his armies to fight the Son of God for supremacy.

We will discuss the who, when, and why of the battle at Armageddon later. First I want to show you ten signs which indicate that we're well on our way there.

1. The Knowledge Explosion

The first road sign pointing toward Armageddon is found in Daniel 12:4: "But you, Daniel, shut up the words, and seal the book until the time of the end; many shall run to and fro, and knowledge shall increase." The literal translation of this Scripture indicates that during the end time, or the terminal generation, an explosion of knowledge will occur.

Just such an explosion has occurred in the last century. From the Garden of Eden until A.D. 1900, men walked or rode horses just as King David and Julius Caesar did. In the span of a few years, however, mankind invented the automobile, the jet plane, and the space shuttle. You can fly from New York to Paris in three hours today. Just think of all the knowledge involved in developing these marvels of modern technology.

Our technology has increased exponentially. Technology, while not necessarily advancing knowledge in the average man or woman, has made fathomless depths of knowledge and information available to us at the press of a button. You can receive faxes in your car, take a message on your sky pager, and explore encyclopedias of vast knowledge small enough to fit in the palm of your hand. You can sit in the quiet of your own home and drown yourself in information from the Internet.

In the last two generations we have put men on the moon and redefined both death and life. Medical science has the ability to keep a corpse breathing for months on life support. Tiny babies weighing less than one pound can survive, and unborn babies can even undergo surgery while within the womb.

All this knowledge ought to be a good thing, but still we're on the road to Armageddon. Our knowledge has not produced utopia; instead it has created a generation of well-informed people who know more about rock stars than history. Our "enlightened" society seeks freedom and self-expression, but is actually enslaved by drugs, perversion, and occult practices.

We favor death for the innocent and mercy for the guilty. We tout the benefits of secular humanism, the worship of man's intellect, yet our enlightened, religion-free government finds itself impotent in the face of growing crime. Why? Because knowledge without God can only produce intellectual barbarians, smarter sinners. Hitler's Nazis threw Jewish children alive into the ovens. Many of them were educated men, some had Ph.D.s, but their education was accomplished without the acknowledgment or the knowledge of God.

We are the terminal generation, "always learning but never able to come to the knowledge of the truth" (2 Tim. 3:7) because we seek truth apart from God. You can't think your way to truth. You can't philosophize your way there. You can't think happy thoughts and find truth. The only way you will ever find eternal, ultimate truth, is by seeking and finding God.

If you reject truth, the only thing left to accept is a lie. America has rejected the truth of God's Word. We have rejected God Himself, and all we have left is the secular humanist lie. But Jesus said, "You shall know the truth, and the truth shall make you free" (John 8:32).

---

2. Plague in the Middle East

My father's generation could not understand several prophetic passages of Scripture. One such prophecy was Zechariah 14:12–15:

> And this shall be the plague with which the LORD will strike all the people who fought against Jerusalem: their flesh shall dissolve while they stand on their feet, their eyes shall dissolve in their sockets, and their tongues shall dissolve in their mouths. It shall come to pass in that day that a great panic from the LORD will be among them. Everyone will seize the hand of his neighbor, and raise his hand against his neighbor's hand; Judah also will fight at Jerusalem. And the wealth of all the surrounding nations shall be gathered together: gold, silver, and apparel in great abundance. Such also shall be the plague on the horse and the mule, on the camel and the donkey, and on all the cattle that will be in those camps. So shall this plague be.

Zechariah had a vision and didn't know how to describe what he saw, so he called the gruesome results a plague. The plague which could consume a man's flesh while he was still standing was as much a mystery to my father's generation as it was to Zechariah. But now we know about the Ebola virus and other deadly, swift diseases. Author Richard Preston describes an Ebola victim in his best-seller, *The Hot Zone:*

> They opened him up for an autopsy and found that his kidneys were destroyed and that his liver was dead. His liver had ceased functioning several days before he died. It was yellow, and parts of it had liquefied—it looked like the liver of a three-day-old cadaver. It was as if [the victim] had become a corpse before his death. Sloughing of the gut, in which the intestinal lining comes off, is another effect that is ordinarily seen in a corpse that is days old. . . . Everything had gone wrong inside this man, absolutely everything, any one of which could have been fatal: the clotting, the massive hemorrhages, the liver turned into pudding, the intestines full of blood.[2]

Preston states that an airborne strain of Ebola could emerge and circle around the world in about six weeks, like the flu, killing large numbers of people.[3] Of course, Ebola doesn't kill a man instantly as does the plague described in the Bible, but in the great influenza epidemic in 1918, people died within hours of first manifesting symptoms. Zechariah's plague could be another virus, one we have not yet seen. Despite our great increase of knowledge, we are not equipped to handle the hantavirus, Ebola, or the host of other "new" mutated viruses that could strike swiftly and severely. If new strains of these viruses were introduced through chemical or biological warfare, we could very well see a plague like the one Zechariah described.

Zechariah's plague could also be the logical result of massive radiation. A docudrama about Hiroshima presented a reenactment of the bombing that ended World War II. Watching the program, I saw flesh literally melting off the bones of the victims before the corpses could hit the ground. Suddenly I understood that Zechariah could have been describing nuclear warfare.

Consider this fact: every military weapon ever invented has been used. After we bombed Japan and ended the second World War, everyone became aware of the atomic bomb's immense power. An A-bomb can produce a temperature of 150 million degrees Fahrenheit in one millionth of a second. Under such conditions, a man's tongue and eyes can be consumed before his corpse can hit the ground.

But we've come a long way since the A-bomb. A one megaton nuclear blast, a firecracker compared to the massive H-bomb, creates a great noise (like the one described in 2 Peter 3:10), instantly atomizing everything within a two-mile radius. For the next eight miles, everything instantly catches fire. The land becomes a raging inferno, a literal hell on earth. Radiation breaks down at thirty-five miles and the earth is good for nothing for a hundred years.

Saddam Hussein, another enemy of Israel, is presently trying desperately to get a nuclear bomb put together to conquer the entire Middle East because he wants to be another Nebuchadnezzar. A U.S. Congressman recently sat in my office and said that many of the nuclear weapons produced by the former Soviet Union have disappeared—we assume that they have been sold to Israel's enemies. And don't forget chemical weapons.

According to a study of chemical weapons by Dr. Danny Shoham of the Begin-Sadat Center for Strategic Studies at Bar-Ilan University, Syria today is the strongest military power in the Arab world in the area of chemical weapons. The Syrians have produced thousands of chemical bombs as well as a well developed delivery capability including both attack planes and Scud-B missiles (100 to 200). Recently the Syrians began producing the longer range Scud-C and possibly the M9 missiles in cooperation with Iran, North Korea and China. Using these longer range missiles, the Syrians will be able to strike literally every point in Israel from any location in Syria.[4]

And even the Patriot missiles used in the Gulf War wouldn't afford much protection for Israel. "In point of fact, as far as Israel is concerned, American technology was a dismal failure during the Gulf War: the Patriot missiles failed to intercept even one Iraqi Scud and American technology failed to destroy or even keep track of the Scud missile sites."[5]

The coming military attack upon Israel will be ferocious and fast. "Let him who is on the housetop not go down to take anything out of his house," the Bible warns. "And let him who is in the field not go back to get his clothes" (Matt. 24:17, 18). Why? There will be *no time*.

Israel, of course, knows that she has enemies. Israel currently has the nuclear capacity to turn the sands of Baghdad into a molten sea of glass if Hussein ever attacks. If you're interested in further reading, I recommend *The Samson Option* by Seymour M. Hirsh (Random House), which describes in detail Israel's nuclear capability.

The *Sunday Times* of London once printed a story given to them by Mordecai Vanunu. Vanunu reported that Israel had two hundred nuclear bombs in addition to the neutron and the H-bomb. After this revelation, Vanunu was immediately arrested by the Mossad and sentenced to eighteen years in prison for a breach of security. His arrest confirmed that he was telling the truth. If he had been lying, the Mossad would have never bothered with him.[6]

Incidentally, we Americans often think that we're somehow protected from nuclear warfare. That is a misguided notion. During the Persian Gulf War, General Schwarzkopf asked President Bush for permission to explode an electromagnetic pulse device high in the heavens. Such a device would have instantly cut off all communication between Saddam Hussein and his troops. Bush did not give his permission, and the device has not yet been tested on the battlefield.[7]

Such a device, known to military strategists as an "electric blanket," sounds like something out of a James Bond movie, but it could easily be used against North America. A satellite carrying a nuclear warhead crossing over America at the height of 450 kilometers (279 miles) would explode, sending out an electronic pulse of enormous energy harmless to humans but fatal to our delicate electronic machines, which are designed to operate with minuscule amounts of energy. In one billionth of a second, all communication would be cut off. Transmissions to cars and trucks and machinery would grind to a halt as their electrical systems fried; radio and television stations would blink off the air. Planes would crash, missile systems would fail, the President and Commander-in-Chief would be unable to communicate with his military forces. Everything that relied on electricity would stop functioning. Military strategists have predicted that in the event of a nuclear war, this is how the enemy will terminate all electrical transmission. Vital to the success of any military system are the "three Cs": command, control, and communication. The "electric blanket" would wreak havoc among an enemy by eliminating all three.

And in addition to all of this, it may be only a matter of time before some terrorist abandons diesel fuel and fertilizer for a nuclear weapon smuggled from the shards of the Soviet Empire and blows up an entire city just to make a political statement.

Nuclear bombs and star wars weapons systems—other irrefutable signs that we are the terminal generation.

---

3. The Rebirth of Israel

I remember very clearly one day when I was eight years old—May 15, 1948. I was sitting at our kitchen table with my father, a quiet man with a brilliant mind. Dad loved books and he was a student of prophecy, but he didn't always do too well with people. He didn't talk much, but when he did speak, what he said was worth hearing.

Dad and I were quietly listening to the radio. Then the newscaster from the radio station made an announcement: "The United Nations has today announced that they have formally recognized the state of Israel."

My father put the book he was holding down on the table and said nothing for a long moment. I knew from the look in his eyes that he had been profoundly moved. Then he looked at me and said, "We have just heard the most important prophetic message that will ever be delivered until Jesus Christ returns to earth."

I've forgotten many episodes from my youth, but I never forgot that night or my father's words. He was right: biblical prophecy states that Israel must experience a rebirth before the coming of her Messiah.

The Bible also prophesies that a nation will be born in a day:

> "Who has heard such a thing? Who has seen such things? Shall the earth be made to give birth in one day? Or shall a nation be born at once? For as soon as Zion was in labor, she gave birth to her children. Shall I bring to the time of birth, and not cause delivery?" says the LORD. "Shall I who cause delivery shut up the womb?" says your God. "Rejoice with Jerusalem, and be glad with her, all you who love her; rejoice for joy with her, all you who mourn for her." (Is. 66:8–10)

The disciples came to Jesus and asked him for the signs of the end of the age. "Tell us," they said, "when will these things be? And what will be the sign of Your coming, and of the end of the age?" (Matt. 24:3).

Jesus responded by saying, "Now learn this parable from the fig tree: When its branch has already become tender and puts forth leaves, you know that summer is near. So you also, when you see all these things, know that it is near—at the doors! Assuredly, I say to you, this generation will by no means pass away till all these things take place" (Matt. 24:32–34).

In Bible prophecy Israel is often pictured as a fig tree. Jesus says, "As soon as its twigs get tender and its leaves come out." His meaning is very clear: when Israel is a young tree, reborn and growing, putting forth leaves, it should be *obvious to all* that the end times are at hand.

Jesus said, "This generation will certainly not pass away until all these things have happened." The generation which sees the rebirth of Israel is the terminal generation.

---

4. The Jews Will Return Home

From A.D. 70, when the Romans attacked Jerusalem, destroyed the Temple, and set into motion a series of events which resulted in the Diaspora, the Jewish people have been scattered throughout the Mediterranean Basin, and from there throughout the entire world. They were not in control of their own destiny, nor did they dwell in a homeland of their own until May 15, 1948.

Jeremiah declared that the Jews must return to Israel before Messiah comes: "'Therefore, behold, the days are coming,' says the LORD, 'that they shall no longer say, "As the LORD lives who brought up the children of Israel from the land of Egypt," but, "As the LORD lives who brought up and led the descendants of the house of Israel from the north country and from all the countries where I had driven them." And they shall dwell in their own land'" (Jer. 23:7, 8).

The Jews from the north country (Russia) have returned to Israel by the tens of thousands, as have Jewish people from around the globe. We have seen them on CNN disembarking from planes in Tel Aviv. We have read it in every form of print media. They do live in their own land, just as Jeremiah predicted. Their return to their homeland is another sign of the terminal generation.

5. Jerusalem No Longer Under Gentile Rule

Biblical prophecy states that Jerusalem will not be under Gentile rule in the terminal generation, a situation which had existed from A.D. 70 until the Six Day War of 1967. Jesus Christ predicted that Jerusalem would be "trampled by the Gentiles until the times of the Gentiles are fulfilled" (Luke 21:24). David the psalmist predicted that the Lord would rebuild Zion and appear in his glory there (see Ps. 102:16).

That's why David wrote, "Pray for the peace of Jerusalem" (Ps. 122:6).

6. International Instant Communication

And I will give power to my two witnesses, and they will prophesy one thousand two hundred and sixty days, clothed in sackcloth. . . . When they finish their testimony, the beast that ascends out of the bottomless pit will make war against them, overcome them, and kill them. And their dead bodies will lie in the street of the great city which spiritually is called Sodom and Egypt, where also our Lord was crucified. Then those from the peoples, tribes, tongues, and nations will see their dead bodies three-and-a-half days, and not allow their dead bodies to be put into graves. And those who dwell on the earth will rejoice over them, make merry, and send gifts to one another, because these two prophets tormented those who dwell on the earth. (Rev. 11:3, 7–10)

The two witnesses, who many theologians believe to be Elijah and Enoch, will appear on the earth during the Tribulation. They wear the traditional clothing of mourning, and their mission will be to call men to repentance.

Prophecy states that the whole world will, at the same time, be able to see the two witnesses in the streets of Jerusalem. My father's generation could not explain that. How could the whole world see two dead men lying in the streets of Jerusalem at one time? It was a mystery.

Then came television, followed by international satellites, the Internet, and wireless communication. In this generation we can see any major news story happening anywhere on the globe within seconds of the event. Virtually the entire world has access to the same information as an event happens. World leaders communicate with each other via CNN, confident that owing to an antenna, a cable, or a satellite dish in some remote place, the other person is watching.

This was not possible in 1900!

This was not possible in 1960!

It is possible today . . . because this could be the terminal generation. The entire population living during the Tribulation will see the two witnesses slain in the streets of Jerusalem, will see the Antichrist, and will see the coming of Messiah.

---

7. Days of Deception

In Matthew 24, Jesus warned, "Take heed that no one deceives you" (v. 4). Bible prophecy declares that deception will be epidemic on the earth in the terminal generation: "Everyone will deceive his neighbor, and will not speak the truth; they have taught their tongue to speak lies; they weary themselves to commit iniquity" (Jer. 9:5).

Deception is going to be the cardinal indicator of the terminal generation, and though deception has always been with us, the coming Antichrist and his "PR man," called the "false prophet" by the apostle John, will elevate deception to an art form. Even the appellation of the Antichrist, "Man of Peace," is a lie.

But the world will be ready for him, eager and willing to believe anything. Why wouldn't it be? For generations we've been cutting our teeth and weakening our wills with lies. Secular humanism is deception, for it holds that man can usurp the role of God. The teaching of situational ethics, the philosophy that there is no absolute right or wrong, has produced a generation riddled with AIDS and abortion-induced guilt.

New Age theories and philosophies are nothing but deception. They are the same lie Satan told Eve: "And you shall be like God." The environmental gurus who teach that the earth is but the breast of "mother goddess" are doling out deception—some of America's finest young men are going out into the woods, ripping off their clothes, hugging a tree, and baying at the moon, trying to discover who they are. That's deception, because you can't find the Creator if you're worshiping the creation.

Satanism and teachings of the occult are nothing but deception. The apostate church, which has a form of godliness but denies the power of God, is peddling sheer deception because it has exchanged the truth of God for a lie (see 2 Tim. 3:5; Rom. 1:25). Such churches deliberately ignore the imminent coming of Christ, saying, "Where is the promise of His coming? For since the fathers fell asleep, all things continue as they were from the beginning of creation" (2 Pet. 3:4).

You can't find truth in the world's best-sellers! What God wants you to know about the future is written in His Book, not in *The Celestine Prophecy.* Run from those who tell lies, and turn your attention to God's truth, lest your senses become dull like others of the terminal generation and you can no longer discern what is true and what is not.

---

8. Famines and Pestilence

America has the ability to feed the world, yet we pay farmers not to grow certain crops lest they glut the market and drive prices down. And every night on television we see footage of starving children with bloated bellies, bulging eyes, and bare ribs. There are many hungry children even in the United States.

The Bible predicted that we would know famine. Jesus said that in the latter days "there will be famines, pestilences, and earthquakes in various places. All these are the beginning of sorrows" (Matt. 24:7, 8).

Another translation calls these signs "the beginning of birth pains" (NIV). Famine, pestilences, and earthquakes are the pains experienced at the birth of the terminal generation. When a woman begins to feel her first sharp pains, she knows the end of her pregnancy is near. The event she's been waiting and praying for is finally upon her.

The Jewish people know about these birth pangs. Hebrew eschatology, called *acharit ha-yamin,* describes the pre-Messianic era as one of great upheavals and wars, known as "the birth pangs of the Messiah," and Jewish suffering and exile.

The *Talmud* describes this era as the "footprints of the Messiah"—a time when arrogance will increase. The government will turn to heresy, and there will be no one to rebuke its wrongdoing. Young people will shame their elders, a person's own family will become his enemies.[8]

Pestilence—incurable disease—is another sign that we have reached the terminal generation. Many years ago I was preaching about pestilence and a man came up later and said, "Look, Pastor Hagee, I've got a bone to pick with you. You said pestilence is incurable disease, but medical science has the ability to control every sickness known to man."

I answered that the Bible said things would change. According to Joshua Lederberg, a Nobel laureate from Rockefeller University, many experts were absolutely confident in the 1960s that medical science had solved forever the problem of infectious diseases. But today, say the medical experts, disease is on the march, and the human race is not now ready to defend itself against what is really "an unending siege by pestilence."[9]

A few years ago we discovered AIDS, the Ebola virus, and antibiotic-resistant bacteria. None of these will be conquered easily. AIDS alone is a medical black hole that has touched the life of practically every American, and after more than a decade of intense research, still virtually everyone who gets it dies.

According to the most recent mortality study conducted by the U.S. Centers for Disease Control and Prevention, AIDS is now the leading cause of death for twenty-five to forty-four year olds and was ranked as the eighth leading cause of death overall for Americans in 1992. Scientists estimate that one million Americans—one in every 250 people—are infected with HIV.[10]

I believe the power of God can heal an AIDS victim, and that's the only real hope those victims have. The answer can't be found in condoms, "safe sex," or even research—the answer is found in obeying the moral laws of God!

AIDS, Ebola, and killer viruses are a trumpet blast from the throne of God to the spiritually deaf . . . *You are the terminal generation!*

9. Earthquakes

Earthquakes are another sign of the last days. Historians of the fifteenth century recorded 115 earthquakes in various places. Two hundred fifty-three earthquakes were recorded in the sixteenth century. There were 378 recorded earthquakes in the seventh century, 640 in the eighteenth, and 2,119 in the nineteenth.[11] Someone might try to explain this away by thinking that there are no more earthquakes today than in the past, and it's just that our ability to detect them has improved. But the number of earthquakes recorded has risen from 2,588 in 1983 to 4,084 in 1992.[12]

Now we are nearing the end of the twentieth century and bracing for the "big one" that is sure to come for Southern California. California is split by the San Andreas Fault while geologists probe the breast of mother earth for any clues that might predict when California might experience the "big one."

The Bible records at least thirty-three instances of God using earthquakes to communicate with the spiritually hard of hearing. The earth quaked at Mount Sinai when Moses received the Ten Commandments (see Ex. 19:18); God used an earthquake in Jerusalem at the crucifixion to split the veil of the temple from the top to the bottom (see Matt. 27:51). He used an earthquake at the resurrection to roll the stone from the borrowed tomb—not to let Jesus out, but to let others in (see Matt. 28:2). He used an earthquake to set Paul and Silas free from the jail at Philippi (see Acts 16:26). And He will announce the coming of Israel's Messiah with an earthquake: "And he said, 'The LORD roars from Zion, and utters His voice from Jerusalem; and the pastures of the shepherds mourn, and the top of Carmel withers'" (Amos 1:2). At the coming of the Messiah, the Dome of the Rock in Jerusalem (if it is still standing) will collapse and Mount of Olives will split in half.

The constant trembling of the earth is God's voice speaking through nature, reminding us that we are the terminal generation.

10. As in the Days of Noah . . .

But of that day and hour no one knows, not even the angels of heaven, but My Father only. But as the days of Noah were, so also will the coming of the Son of Man be. For as in the days before the flood, they were eating and drinking, marrying and giving in marriage, until the day that Noah entered the ark, and did not know until the flood came and took them all away, so also will the coming of the Son of Man be. (Matt. 24:36–39)

What characteristics marked the "days of Noah"? Genesis tells us that man's wickedness on the earth was very great and that "every intent of the thoughts of his heart was only evil continually" (Gen. 6:5).

If you open your morning paper at breakfast tomorrow, you're likely to lose your appetite. Murders, rapes, kidnapping, assault, child abuse, spouse abuse, parental abuse—these are common headlines for even small town newspapers. Men are thinking evil all the time. And just as the flood waters caught them unaware, so the end of the earth will catch these deceived sleepers. The Messiah will come, the thread of history will snap, and those who were unprepared will be caught up in the Tribulation which is to follow.

CHAPTER SIX

What Is the Rapture and When Will It Happen?

K nowing this first: that scoffers will come in the last days, walking according to their own lusts" (2 Pet. 3:3). The simple fact that we hear voices denying the certainty of a literal Rapture is, in and of itself, another sign that we are the terminal generation.

Listen to the writers of the Bible as they describe this incredible, soon-coming event: 1 Thessalonians 4:16–18 says, "For the Lord Himself will descend from heaven with a shout, with the voice of an archangel, and with the trumpet of God. And the dead in Christ [Christians who have died] will rise first. Then we who are alive and remain shall be caught up together with them in the clouds to meet the Lord in the air. And thus we shall always be with the Lord. Therefore comfort one another with these words."

Matthew 24:30 says, "Then the sign of the Son of Man will appear in heaven, and then all the tribes of the earth will mourn, and they will see the Son of Man coming on the clouds of heaven with power and great glory."

In Acts 1:11, after Jesus had ascended into heaven, an angel appeared and spoke to the stunned disciples: "'Men of Galilee, why do you stand gazing up into heaven?' the angel said. 'This same Jesus, who was taken up from you into heaven, will so come in like manner as you saw Him go into heaven.'"

"For as the lightning comes from the east and flashes to the west, so also will the coming of the Son of Man be" (Matt. 24:27).

Put these verses together and we have this picture: Jesus Christ, the Prince of Glory, will appear suddenly in the heavens, brilliantly, in a way that no one will be able to miss.

When I was attending graduate school at North Texas State University, I was in the library doing research for a term paper when a book dealing with weather patterns attracted my attention. I took the book off the shelf, dusted it off, and began to read. One section that dealt with storms caught my eye, and one specific line seemed to leap off the page: "When lightening flashes from the east to the west, you can be sure the storm is over."

When Jesus Christ, the Light of the World, appears in the heavens as lightning flashing from the east to the west, the storms of life will be over for the believer.

A Mystery

In 1 Corinthians 15:51–52, Paul writes, "Behold, I tell you a mystery: We shall not all sleep, but we shall all be changed—in a moment, in the twinkling of an eye, at the last trumpet. For the trumpet will sound, and the dead will be raised incorruptible, and we shall be changed."

Paul addressed this problem because the people of the New Testament Church were beginning to die—and they had fully expected Jesus Christ to come back to earth for them before any of them passed away. So Paul shares with them a "mystery," a term used in Scripture to denote something God has not previously chosen to share with men. They wanted to know what would happen after death. Would those who died have a part in the eternal kingdom to come?

Paul answered their questions by explaining the mystery of things to come. Believers who had died would not miss the

Savior's coming, Paul told them, but would come out of the grave at the sound of the trumpet to be raised incorruptible, with a new, supernatural, immortal body. Those who had not yet died a physical death would be caught up in the clouds to meet Jesus Christ. This mass ingathering of believers is commonly called the Rapture.

Now if you were to ask ordinary church members in America what they thought of the Rapture, far too many would look at you with puzzled expressions on their faces. Many have never heard the word mentioned from their pulpits and haven't the foggiest idea what the word means.

Many evangelical churches have preached the doctrine of the Rapture for years, but now even they are under attack for teaching that a literal gathering of the church will occur. More liberal theologians are even shouting in chorus, "There will never be a Rapture!"

But what does the Word of God say?

When and How Will Jesus Come for the Believers?

Jesus said, "But of that day and hour no one knows, not even the angels in heaven, nor the Son, but only the Father" (Mark 13:32). Despite the thousands of people who would like to predict the exact year, month, date, or hour of Christ's return, Jesus said no man knows. But God the Father knows when He will send Jesus to fetch His bride home, and when He gives the word, Jesus will leave the right hand of the Father and descend through the clouds to gather in His church.

Immediately following Jesus' appearing in the heavens, the trumpet of God will sound, announcing the appearance of royalty, for He is the Prince of Peace, the Lord of Glory, the King of Kings and the Lord of all Lords. The voice of the archangel will summon the dead from their graves and all over the earth the graves of those who have trusted Christ as their Messiah will explode as their occupants soar into the heavens to meet the Light of the World. Marble mausoleums will topple as the bodies of resurrected saints rise to meet the Lord. Cars will empty beside the interstate, their engines running, their drivers and occupants strangely missing. Supper dishes will steam in the homes of believers, food will boil on their stoves, but no one will remain to eat this earthly dinner, for all believers will be taking their places at the heavenly table for the marriage supper of the Lamb.

The next day, headlines of local, national, and international newspapers will scream, "MILLIONS MISSING WITH NO EXPLANATION." New Age devotees might explain the mass disappearance by insisting that a vast armada of UFOs have abducted millions of people.

TV stations will broadcast live from local neighborhoods and cemeteries, and their cameras will capture empty graves, ruptured mausoleums, silent homes, wrecked cars. They'll interview neighbors who dab their eyes with tissue and exclaim, "I was right here talking to Mr. Jones and suddenly he disappeared. Right in front of my eyes, I tell you. He was here— and then he vaporized! Like something out of *Star Trek,* but faster!"

Nightline will feature a panel of esteemed educators, philosophers, and clergymen who will attempt to explain what has happened. The token psychologist will declare that the world is experiencing unprecedented mass hysteria. The venerable theologian will jabber about "right-wing, Bible-thumping, politically incorrect hate-mongers" who believed an invalid and nonsensical theory about something called the Rapture.

Yet there is one person who will have an explanation for the Rapture that will satisfy many of those who are left behind—his name will be Antichrist.

Telephone lines around the world will jam as families try to check on their loved ones. And the churches of the world will be packed with weeping, hysterical people who see the truth too late and cry, "The Lord of Glory has come and we are left behind to go through the Tribulation and to face the coming Antichrist."

What is the Rapture? It is the literal ingathering of the Church as explained clearly in the Word of God. It's the only way to fly!

Signs of an Imminent Rapture

Jesus Christ, the Messiah for Jews and Gentiles alike, first came to earth nearly two thousand years ago. He will come to earth again when He sets foot on the Mount of Olives just outside Jerusalem, but He will appear briefly to gather his church before the Antichrist, or the "man of lawlessness" is revealed:

> Let no one deceive you by any means; for that Day will not come unless the falling away comes first, and the man of sin is revealed, the son of perdition, who opposes and exalts himself above all that is called God or that is worshiped, so that he sits as God in the temple of God, showing himself that he is God.
>
> Do you not remember that when I was still with you I told you these things? And now you know what is restraining, that he may be revealed in his own time. For the mystery of lawlessness is already at work; only He who now restrains will do so until He is taken out of the way. And then the lawless one will be revealed, whom the Lord will consume with the breath of His mouth and destroy with the brightness of His coming. The coming of the lawless one is according to the working of Satan, with all power, signs, and lying wonders, and with all unrighteous deception among those who perish, because they did not receive the love of the truth, that they might be saved. (2 Thess. 2:3–10)

According to Paul, author of the letters to the believers at Thessalonica, the Antichrist cannot be revealed until the One who holds back the power of sin and lawlessness is taken out of the way. The One who restrains sin is the Holy Spirit, the One who indwells every member of the sanctified Church, those who have trusted Jesus Christ as their Lord and Savior, the One who right now is continuously convicts the world of sin, righteousness, and judgment (see John 16:8–11).

How is the Holy Spirit removed from the earth? This will occur when those who have placed their faith and trust in Jesus Christ are snatched away. This momentous event, which will occur in "the twinkling of an eye," could happen at any time. No one knows the day or the hour. As they did when Noah was building the ark, people on earth will be conducting their daily affairs, eating and drinking, marrying and giving in marriage, buying and selling. And just as God set apart his chosen ones by placing Noah and his family into the ark for safekeeping, He will remove his set-apart Church from the seven years of tribulation to come.

The Importance of Understanding the Rapture

Some of you may be tempted to ask, "Pastor Hagee, what difference does it make? I'm not going to change the way I live whether the Rapture is coming or not."

Friend, the truth and implications of the Rapture are not take-it-or-leave-it teachings. The Bible says, "Watch therefore, and pray always that you may be counted worthy to escape all these things that will come to pass, and to stand before the Son of Man" (Luke 21:36), and "The end of all things is at hand; therefore be serious and watchful in your prayers" (1 Pet. 4:7). Also, in the parable of the five wise virgins and the five foolish virgins, Jesus urges us to be ready for the appearance of the bridegroom (see Matt. 25:1–13).

If you want to go with Him, you need to be watching for Him.

We need to be watching, praying, ever-ready for the appearance of Jesus Christ to gather those who believe in Him. We can't get too comfortable with the things of this world because, as the Scriptures say,

> [We] are a chosen people, a royal priesthood, a holy nation, a people belonging to God, that [we] may declare the praises of him who called [us] out of darkness into his wonderful light. Once [we] were not a people, but now [we] are the people of God; once [we] had not received mercy, but now [we] have received mercy. Dear friends, I urge you, *as aliens and strangers in the world, to abstain from sinful desires, which war against your soul.* Live such good lives among the pagans that, though they accuse you of doing wrong, they may see your good deeds and glorify God on the day he visits us. (1 Pet. 2:9–12 NIV, emphasis mine)

The Heavenly Wedding Reception

In the "twinkling of an eye" all the believers in Jesus the Messiah from throughout the church age will stand in the heavens. The bride of Christ, the Church, will gather there, ten thousand times ten thousands of us. God shall wipe away every tear. That, my fellow Christian, will be our heavenly reunion. We'll have supernatural, incorruptible bodies which will no longer know suffering, disease, or pain. I will stand before God's throne with my father, my mother, my grandparents, and hundreds of dear saints who went before me into Heaven. The saints of Christ will be wearing crowns and dazzling white robes of righteousness, for we are the bride, adorned for our wedding with Christ, our heavenly groom.

Through his grace, we His bride will stand before our Bridegroom Jesus and offer to Him our dowry, the things we have done in His name. These works do not buy our entrance into heaven, but we offer them in love, as gifts from a loving Church to a waiting Savior. And for our efforts, we may receive as many as six crowns:

- The crown for those who love His appearance (2 Tim. 4:8): "Finally, there is laid up for me the crown of righteousness, which the Lord, the righteous Judge, will give to me on that Day, and not to me only but also to all who have loved [earnestly longed for] His appearing."

- The crown for enduring trials (James 1:12): "Blessed is the man who endures temptation; for when he has been approved, he will receive the crown of life which the Lord has promised to those who love Him."

- The crown for those willing to feed the flock (1 Pet. 5:2–4): "Shepherd the flock of God which is among you, serving as overseers, not by compulsion but willingly, not for dishonest gain but eagerly; nor as being lords over those entrusted to you, but being examples to the flock; and when the Chief Shepherd appears, you will receive the crown of glory that does not fade away."

- The crown for those who are faithful unto death (Rev. 2:10): "Do not fear any of those things which you are about to suffer. Indeed, the devil is about to throw some of you into prison, that you may be tested, and you will have tribulation ten days. Be faithful until death, and I will give you the crown of life."

- The crown for those who win souls (1 Thess. 2:19): "For what is our hope, or joy, or crown of rejoicing? Is it not even you in the presence of our Lord Jesus Christ at His coming?"

- The crown for those who master the old nature (1 Cor. 9:24–25): "Do you not know that those who run in a race all run, but one receives the prize? Run in such a way that you may obtain it. And everyone who competes for the prize is temperate in all things. Now they do it to obtain a perishable crown, but we for an imperishable crown."

Once we have received our crowns, we will sit at the wedding feast prepared for the bride of Christ. The Church, the body of believers, is the bride without spot or wrinkle, the bride purchased with the blood of Jesus, the Lamb of God who died for us and in our place to pay the penalty for our sins. That dinner will be a glorious celebration, for the bride has been victorious over the powers and principalities of darkness. We, the members of His raptured Church, were the salt and light of the earth, the pure in heart, the peacemakers, the ones who endured persecution in Jesus' name.

If you listen closely, you can almost hear the orchestra of heaven beginning to play the wedding march.

Don't Be Fooled by a False Groom

Think about it! Anyone can stand on the Mount of Olives in Jerusalem and say, "I am Jesus." Anyone can wear a white robe. Anyone can claim to be the descendant of King David and have his followers crown him as the king of the new Israel on Jerusalem's temple mount. Anyone could place surgical scars in his hands and feet. There are warlocks and witch doctors on the earth right now who can call fire from heaven and perform miracles. You can turn on your television and watch "healers" do bloodless surgery with their fingernails. Remember this: a man with supernatural power is not necessarily from God. The devil has supernatural power, too, as do his demons.

How are you going to recognize the real Jesus? Jesus said, "Then if anyone says to you, 'Look, here is the Christ!' or 'There!' do not believe it" (Matt. 24:23). The world is full of false messiahs and false Christs, and during the Tribulation, God will send a powerful spirit of delusion:

> The coming of the lawless one [Antichrist] is according to the working of Satan, with all power, signs, and lying wonders, and with all unrighteous deception among those who perish, because they did not receive the love of the truth, that they might be saved. And for this reason God will send them strong delusion, that they should believe the lie, that they all may be condemned who did not believe the truth but had pleasure in unrighteousness. (2 Thess. 2:9–12)

In the eighties *USA Today* ran a full page ad that read, "Christ Is Now on the Earth." The *New York Times* carried a similar ad proclaiming, "Christ is Now Here." Those ads ran in the early eighties, and I threw them away after showing them on national television. Christ isn't on the earth in bodily form, for when He comes again, the entire world will know about it!

Once one of our church members told me, "Pastor Hagee, a lady told me she was driving in California and suddenly Jesus appeared in the car with her. What do you think?"

"I'll tell you what I think," I answered. "I don't believe it."

Jesus is not in California, New York, or Rome. He is seated at the right hand of God the Father, where He will stay until Gabriel blows the trumpet to call the dead in Christ from their dusty couches of slumber to mansions on high.

Let me ask again: How will you be able to tell the real Jesus from the false pretenders? Jesus knew and prophesied that many pretenders would come saying, "I am Christ." So God installed a fail-safe mechanism that is so staggering in supernatural power, so earth-shattering, that not even Satan himself could imitate it, much less duplicate it. That fail-safe method is the Rapture!

Satan has always tried to imitate whatever God does. In the Old Testament, Jannes and Jambres imitated Moses (see 2 Tim. 3:8 and Ex. 7:10–12). When Moses threw his rod down and it became a serpent, they threw their rods down and their rods became serpents too. But when Moses' snake consumed their snakes, Jehovah God was demonstrating that He will not be outwitted or overcome by Satan's imitations.

But still Satan tries to deceive. The Antichrist will seek to imitate and ultimately supplant Jesus Christ. In Revelation 6:2 we see that the Antichrist makes his appearance on the world stage riding a white horse:

> "And I looked, and behold, a white horse. He who sat on it had a bow; and a crown was given to him, and he went out conquering and to conquer." [The Antichrist makes this kind of glorious entrance because Jesus Christ comes to earth the second time on a white horse:] "Now I saw heaven opened, and behold, a white horse. And He who sat on him was called Faithful and True, and in righteousness He judges and makes war." (Rev. 19:11)

How will you know when the real Jesus comes to earth? He won't take out an ad in the *New York Times*. He won't speak through some theologian or some charismatic personality who stands on the Mount of Olives or Hollywood Boulevard in a white suit proclaiming that he is the king of the new Israel. He won't come through some warlock who calls down fire from heaven.

I'll know Jesus has reappeared when my glorified body sails through the heavens past the Milky Way into the presence of God. I'll know I'm with the real Jesus when I stand in His glorious presence with my brand new disease-proof, never-dying, fatigue-free body that looks better, feels better, and is better than Arnold Schwarzenegger's.

What Skeptics Say

Those who attack the doctrine of the Rapture are usually those who teach that the Bible is not to be taken literally. Some honor the Word of God in their hearts but nevertheless insist that what is important is the spiritual meaning of Bible passages, which often transcends (and sometimes conflicts with) the literal words themselves. But if you abandon the plain meaning of the text, how do you have any way of evaluating what the "spiritual meaning" is? And thus they face the possibility of giving Scripture a "private interpretation," which is explicitly warned against: "And so we have the prophetic word confirmed, which you do well to heed as a light that shines in a dark place, until the day dawns and the morning star rises in your hearts; knowing this first, that no prophecy of Scripture is of any private interpretation, for prophecy never came by the will of man, but holy men of God spoke as they were moved by the Holy Spirit" (2 Pet. 1:19–21).

Still others who have no more regard for the Word of God than for *Politically Correct Bedtime Stories* insist that whatever meaning the Scriptures have is allegorical at best. But if the Bible is only a collection of fables and allegories, it's a myth and not fit for human consumption—let alone consideration.

Why would God bother to give us a collection of allegories? There is no answer for this because He gave us no such book. The Bible I revere is a literal book from cover to cover, meant to be understood and acted on, not deciphered and dismissed. This is just like God, who, as Augustine somewhere said, "caught orators by fishermen—not fishermen by orators." Consider the following:

- Jesus was literally born of a virgin named Mary.

- He was literally born in Bethlehem.

- He literally healed people.

- He literally died on the cross.

- He literally was buried in a borrowed grave.

- He literally rose from the dead on the third day.

If those things are *literally* true, why shouldn't He *literally* come back to earth with power and great glory? Why shouldn't the Bible be literally true when it says that "every knee should bow . . . and that every tongue should confess that Jesus Christ is Lord, to the glory of God the Father" (Phil. 2:10–11)?

Why shouldn't I literally rise and meet Him in the air as will every believer who looks for His glorious appearing?

Why shouldn't I literally walk on streets of gold? Why shouldn't I literally wear a crown of life? Why shouldn't I literally live forever and forever? Why shouldn't there be a New Jerusalem? Why shouldn't those who are looking for Him literally walk through its gates shouting, "Glory!"?

Critics of the Rapture doctrine are quick to point out that the word *Rapture* does not appear in the Bible. That's absolutely true. The Bible does not contain the term *Trinity* either, but over and over it refers to the "oneness" of God and the "threeness" of God:

1 Corinthians 8:6: "There is but one God, the Father, from whom all things came and for whom we live" (NIV).

Ephesians 4:6: "One God and Father of all, who is above all, and through all, and in you all."

Matthew 28:19: "Go therefore and make disciples of all the nations, baptizing them in the name of the Father and of the Son and of the Holy Spirit."

John 14:26: "But the Helper, the Holy Spirit, whom the Father will send in My name, He will teach you all things, and bring to your remembrance all things that I said to you."

John 15:26: "But when the Helper comes, whom I shall send to you from the Father, the Spirit of truth who proceeds from the Father, He will testify of Me."

2 Corinthians 13:14: "The grace of the Lord Jesus Christ, and the love of God, and the communion of the Holy Spirit be with you all. Amen."

1 Peter 1:2: "According to the foreknowledge of God the Father, in sanctification of the Spirit, for obedience and sprinkling of the blood of Jesus Christ: Grace to you and peace be multiplied."

Though the term *Trinity* isn't in the Bible, the truth of God's three-in-one nature is. The same is true with the truth of the Rapture: the *term* itself isn't in Scripture but the *truth* most certainly is.

Other critics of the Rapture say, "The Rapture teaching is nothing but escapism. You people are trying to escape from the real world." Right now I'm living in the real world, and if I wanted to escape it, I could think of no better way than working and waiting for the coming of my Lord. But I'm thrilled that Jesus Christ is my Lord and Savior, heaven is my home, and that I'm not going to walk in the fires of an eternal hell. If that's escapism, so be it.

Let's face it, everyone wants to escape from something. Environmentalists want to escape from pollution. The people in peace movements want to escape from war. The Bible teaches us to prepare for our escape: "Watch therefore, and pray always that you may be counted worthy to escape all these things that will come to pass, and to stand before the Son of Man" (Luke 21:36).

God Will Rapture His Church to Allow Escape from Tribulation

What does the Rapture allow us to escape? The Tribulation to come. Walk with me through the pages of Revelation chapters six, eight, nine, and sixteen, and let me briefly describe the living hell you will escape by being part of the Rapture:

These are but a few of the things that will happen during the Tribulation:

- One-fourth of mankind will die (see Rev. 6:8), some because of war, some because of famine, and still others by the wild beasts of the earth. Whether by death that is swift and instant or death that is lingering and excruciating—25 percent of all people will die. Now the world's population in 1995 is 5,733,687,096, so a quarter of this is 1,433,421,774 or almost five and a half times the current population of the United States—can you imagine that? And remember that the population of the world is doubling every 39.5 years. So every day the number of people who will die becomes larger and larger.[1]

- One third of all vegetation will be burned up. All grass, every tree, everything green will be destroyed (see Rev. 8:7).

- The sun and the moon will be darkened as nature goes into revolt (see Rev. 8:12).

- The gates of hell will open and hordes of locusts, the size of horses, will come upon the earth. Those locusts will be allowed to sting men like scorpions and the pain will last for five months. The Bible says men will beg God to let them die but they will not die (see Rev. 9:3–6).

- There will be worldwide famine unlike anything the world has ever seen (see Rev. 18:8).

- There will be a world war so bloody that the blood of those killed in battle will flow for two hundred miles up to the bridle of a horse in the valley of Jezreel. This will be the Battle of Armageddon. During the Great Tribulation, one third of all the people on the earth will be killed (see Rev. 14:20).

- Every person on earth will be covered with great running, festering boils. Have you ever had one boil? Imagine being covered in them, not being able to walk, lie down, or sit without pain (see Rev. 16:2–11).

- The seven seas of the earth will be turned into blood. Every river, every stream will become as blood. Every basin in your home will run with hot and cold blood. This plague will produce mind-numbing thirst from which there will be no relief (see Rev. 8:8, 11:6).

- The sun will scorch the earth and men with fire. Major uncontrollable fires will break out all over the world, spontaneously destroying homes, vegetation, and livestock (see Rev. 16:8).

- Mighty men, kings, and men of power will gnaw their tongues in pain and crawl into caves and beg God to kill them (see Rev. 6:15).

- The earth will quake so severely that the islands of the sea will disappear. Puerto Rico and Hawaii will be covered with water. Every building, every wall will crumble. Millions will be trapped beneath the rubble with no one to come to their aid (see Rev. 16:18).

Now I ask you, do you want to escape the coming Tribulation? I do! And I am going to escape. When the archangel blows the trumpet and the dead in Christ rise immediately, those of us who are still alive when Jesus the Messiah returns will rise into the air in the twinkling of an eye to trade the coming hell on earth for the wonder and majesty of heaven. We will meet the real Jesus. He is the Lion of the tribe of Judah. He is the Lord of glory. He is the Light of the world, the Lamb of God, and the Lover of my soul.

The literal, physical appearance of Jesus Christ will come soon. And as soon as the Church is gone, the Antichrist, the son of Satan, will appear upon the stage of the world.

CHAPTER SEVEN

The Coming Antichrist

J esus warned that the times of the Antichrist will be by far the worst the world has ever known. In his discourse to the disciples regarding "the tribulation of those days" as recorded in Matthew 24, Mark 13, Luke 21, and John 16, He foretold of a period of false messiahs, rumors of war, sorrow, betrayal, deceit, iniquity, persecution, and catastrophe. The end times would bring conditions so terrible that "unless those days were shortened, no flesh would be saved" (Matt. 24:22).

Who Is the Antichrist, the False Man of Peace?

The Antichrist will be a man who makes his debut upon the stage of world history with hypnotic charm and charisma. He will probably come from the European Union or a country or confederation that was once part of the Roman Empire, which stretched from Ireland to Egypt and included Turkey, Iran, and Iraq. In Daniel's vision, the "little horn" sprouted among the other ten, which we know are somehow ten divisions of the old Roman Empire. In his rise to power, the Antichrist will weave his hypnotic spell, first over one nation in the ten-kingdom federation, then over all ten. He will conquer three of the ten nations and then assume primacy over all of them; next he will turn his ravenous eyes toward the Apple of God's eye—Israel.

The Antichrist will be a man who has "paid his dues" in the military and the political sense, and many will willingly follow him. He will rule over those in his federation with absolute authority and will do as he pleases (see Dan. 11:36).

We also know that the Antichrist will enter the world stage with a reputation of being a powerful man of peace. Perhaps he will be a Nobel Peace Prize winner. He will defeat and merge three kingdoms—could they be Serbia, Bosnia, and Croatia? Certainly that would be a modern-day miracle. Anyone who could bring peace and unification to the centuries-old strife of that region would surely be known as the greatest man of peace in the modern era. Daniel 8:25 says that by peace he "shall destroy many." He will guarantee peace for Israel and the Middle East and sign a seven-year peace treaty, but will break that seven-year treaty in only three and one-half years (see Dan. 9:27). His peace is neither eternal nor true.

First John 2:18 boldly declares, "Little children, it is the last hour; and as you have heard that the Antichrist is coming, even now many antichrists have come, by which we know that it is the last hour." The Antichrist—capital A—is coming. Though many people throughout the years have been anti-Christ, there is coming a man who is the devil incarnate, the son of Satan, evil personified.

The Antichrist's three-point plan for world domination consists of a one-world economic system in which no one can buy nor sell without a mark sanctioned by the Antichrist's administration; a one-world government, now being called "The New World Order"; and a one-world religion that will eventually focus its worship on the Antichrist himself.

The One-World Economy

The Antichrist's economy will be a cashless society in which every financial transaction can be electronically monitored. John, author of the book of Revelation, described the situation: "He causes all, both small and great, rich and poor, free and slave, to receive a mark on their right hand or on their foreheads, and that no one may buy or sell except one who has the mark or the name of the beast, or the number of his name" (Rev. 13:16–17).

The cashless society may ostensibly be presented to the world as a way to control drug lords, tax evaders, and the like, and so it will be. It may be presented as a foolproof way to end theft or as the ultimate in convenience for the shopper who can go to the supermarket without even a wallet. He will simply have his hand or forehead scanned by an electronic device that reflects the amount of cash he has in the bank, makes the deduction for his purchase, and gives him a current balance.

This scenario doesn't sound nearly as far-fetched as it used to, does it? My bank today offers a debit card; even today I don't need money to go to the grocery store. Everything is scanned these days, from library cards to thumbprints, and it doesn't require a great leap of imagination to see how this cashless, computerized system of buying and selling will be placed into operation. A day is coming when you will not even be able to buy Rolaids without the proper approval, without having a mark upon your hand or forehead scanned.

The computer revolution has made this phenomenal accomplishment well within our grasp. We have become accustomed to being managed by government with numbers. Our children are routinely assigned Social Security numbers by the time they are two years old. Why not make things easier and cut down on the likelihood of fraud by invisibly tattooing a person's identification number or implanting a computer chip beneath the skin of their foreheads or hands?

Because I'm on television, people bring me all sorts of things. A scientist recently brought to my office a box marked "Top Secret." Inside that box was a sample of computer chips that could be implanted in a person's hand or forehead and could contain every fact the government would care to know about an individual. This type of microchip implantation has been done with race horses and other animals for years. Why couldn't it be done with humans?

American politicians are now talking about implementing a national identity card, ostensibly to cut down on illegal aliens. Our government is putting on a full-court press that will ultimately give them the power to control cash transactions.

We are not alone. The European Union is also considering a universal monetary system. *Time* magazine notes, "One month after the latest monetary crisis, Cabinet officers, legislators and bankers on both sides of the Atlantic are intensely debating a lengthening list of ideas" for developing "a global financial system."

The signs are all around us. Bank America has advertised the slogan, "The whole world welcomes world money." A Reader's Digest article entitled "Coming Soon: Electronic Money" claimed that millions of Americans are already receiving their wages and salaries electronically via direct bank deposits. We allow people to automatically draft our bank accounts for loan payments, insurance payments, and many other bills.

I believe the main reason the Antichrist will cause everyone to receive what is known as the "mark of the beast" is to control everyone and crush all who worship the God of Abraham, Isaac, and Jacob. If he cannot personally have the joy of controlling or killing them, he will have the satisfaction of knowing they will starve to death. Without his mark no one will be able to buy a loaf of bread or a drop of milk. They may not be able to buy homes or make rent payments. They may not be able to hold jobs.

The New World Order

Never in the world's history has one government completely ruled the world, but the false man of peace will "devour the whole earth" (Dan. 7:23). He will rule over them by their own consent and with absolute and total authority (see Dan. 11:36). His personality will be marked by great intelligence, persuasiveness, subtlety, and craft. His mouth "speaks pompous words" (Daniel 7:8), and he is a "master of intrigue" (Dan. 8:23 NIV). He will be the world's most prominent, powerful, and popular personality.

The Antichrist will set up a one-world government, a new world order. And believe me, there's nothing new about this new world order! Satan has been scheming to institute one ever since Nimrod proposed to build a mighty tower on the plains of Shinar. The purpose of what we know as the Tower of Babel was to defy God's authority on Earth—to cast God out and institute the government of man. While God commanded men to "Be fruitful and multiply, and fill the earth," (Gen. 9:1), the people had a different idea:

> Now the whole earth had one language and one speech. And it came to pass, as they journeyed from the east, that they found a plain in the land of Shinar, and they dwelt there. . . . And they said, "Come, let us build ourselves a city, and a tower whose top is in the heavens; let us make a name for ourselves, lest we be scattered abroad over the face of the whole earth." (Genesis 11:1–2, 4)

God endured the builders' brashness for a limited time, then he scattered them across the earth.

After World War I, "the war to end all wars," President Woodrow Wilson crafted the League of Nations to uphold peace through a one-world government. Adolph Hitler told the German people he would bring a "new order" to Europe. He did, dragging Europe into the bowels of a living hell and turning the streets crimson with rivers of human blood.

The communists of the former Soviet Union pledged to institute a new world order and erected an atheistic empire that has now collapsed like a house of cards.[1] Now the United Nations wants to establish a new world order!

What does it mean? Brock Chisolm, Director of the United Nations World Health Organization, says, "To achieve world government, it is necessary to remove from the minds of men their individualism, loyalty to their families, national patriotism, and religion."

Destruction of Nationalism and Patriotism

Notice that in essence he called national patriotism and religion enemies of the new world order. Historically, it's interesting to note that George Washington, the father of our country, connected patriotism and religion. He said, "It is impossible to rightly govern the world without God and the Bible. Do not ever let anyone claim to be a true American patriot if they ever attempt to separate religion from politics."[2]

What has happened to American patriotism? I believe it has been slowly dying since the Korean War. That war was officially not our war at all, but a United Nations "police action." Our objective was not total victory; it was repelling the North Koreans without provoking the Chinese and Soviets. General Douglas MacArthur, who resigned at the request of President

Harry Truman, said, "In war, there is no substitute for victory."[3] History has proven MacArthur right.

The Vietnam War was a controlled war. We were not allowed to invade Hanoi. For years we were forbidden to attack the enemy in Laos. The result? America was portrayed to the world as a military loser, incompetent and impotent.

We were in the Gulf as part of the United Nations force by our own insistence; we are in Bosnia as part of NATO at the request of the UN by our own insistence. It is through these kinds of things that many are learning to think of themselves as citizens of the world first and citizens of America second, if at all. Quietly and with great subtlety, the road is being paved for the one-world government of the Antichrist.

Destruction of Evangelical Faith

Underneath the facade of popular peacemaker, the Antichrist will be evil incarnate. He will hate all things of God and will take pleasure in perverting God's intentions. He will rant and rave against God, publicly and privately; he will persecute Christians and Jews alike. He will reject all previous laws, particularly those based on Judeo-Christian values, and institute his own lawless system: "He will speak against the Most High and oppress his saints and try to change the set times and the laws" (Dan. 7:25 NIV).

Every single new world order, including the coming Antichrist's, has had one common trait: an attempt to cast God out of the affairs of men. Why?

As long as we believe the Word of God and are loyal to the kingdom of God, we represent a government within a government. We are pilgrims and strangers who worship another King and have another citizenship, and as such, we are a hindrance to the New World Order. When our government condones what God condemns, those who have trusted in

Him become the enemy. And so the Bible-believing Christians of America are labeled dangerous, "intolerant," and enemies of the state.

Or even freeloaders. A group of people in Colorado has been circulating petitions to place on the ballot an initiative that would call for churches and other nonprofit organizations to pay property tax on their land. But the resolution would not apply to all nonprofit groups. One man explained it this way: "The measure would exempt certain nonprofits, such as schools and charities, that perform necessary community duties. However, other tax-exempt groups, including religious organizations and fraternal lodges, have vast holdings of properties but pay nothing for fire and police protection or infrastructure, nor do they contribute to the public schools."[4] In other words, unlike some institutions that "perform necessary community duties," churches that perform such unimportant functions as preaching salvation, caring for the sick, clothing the naked, feeding the hungry, educating the ignorant, and setting the prisoner free are little more than parasites, and the church is nothing more than a Moose Lodge with a cross on it. This is what the Church of Jesus Christ looks like to those who, as a result of rejecting Jesus the Messiah, have become futile in their thoughts and foolish in their hearts (see Rom. 1:21).

Christian bashing is already an art form in the popular media. Christians are the only group in America that it is politically correct to hate, discriminate against, and lampoon. We are attacked through the law, through the media, through Hollywood, and through educational institutions that belittle the Word of God and traditional family values. When is the last time you saw a heroic, Bible-believing contemporary character on a television show? I can't think of a single instance of twentieth-century faith in God being portrayed as a positive thing. The few good examples of faithful TV characters I can recall are those from shows set in the pioneer days, and their faith is presented as a sentimental quality of the past.

No other group of people on the earth are so constantly maligned on prime-time television. Persistent portrayals of Christians and clergymen as lechers, murderers, and psychopaths betray the deep-seated hostility the media has toward Christianity and faith in God. Perhaps TBS mogul Ted Turner articulated the unverbalized values of his peers when he confided to the TV critic of the *Dallas Morning News:* "Christianity is religion for losers."[5] Imagine what would happen if he said this about Judaism or Islam!

And it goes on and on. National Public Radio commentator Andrei Codrescu described the return of Christ and Christian theology (in 1 Thess. 4:17) as "crap." According to a December 19 transcript of National Public Radio's *All Things Considered*, Codrescu said, "The evaporation of four million [people] who believe in this crap would leave the world in an instantly better place."[6] If Codrescu had said that about Muslims, he would join Salman Rushdie in perpetual hiding to avoid the *fatwa* that would be issued against him. If he had said it about Jews or blacks or homosexuals, he would have been banished from the airwaves forever. But here in America, not only can Codrescu say these things, he can also count on your tax dollars to subsidize his message of hate.

The Antichrist's one-world government will persecute all those who believe in God. This is not at all far-fetched; in fact the handwriting is already on the wall. The American Bar Association, the foremost legal fraternity in America, offered sessions on "How to sue the church through tort law" at its national 1993 convention in San Francisco. In Colorado it looks as if there will be a state law passed under the banner of "hate crimes." No one serious about glorifying God could harbor the cancer of hatred within his soul, but these hate crimes bills are more like a Trojan horse because, as written, they give the state the power to put people in jail for expressing what could be interpreted as their first amendment religious rights—among other things, these laws could be twisted to forbid speaking negatively about a person's "sexual preference."

For instance, if a rabbi or minister told his congregation that homosexuality is an abomination before God—which Scripture says it is—he could be fined and thrown in jail. As America slides deeper into the slime of secular humanism, I believe the law will eventually be interpreted in this way.

Consider the attack being made against religion in the public schools of America. When my son, Matthew, was in the third grade, his teacher asked the class to write a two-paragraph story about Christmas. Because his mother is Hispanic, Matthew chose to write about Christmas in Mexico. He described *Las Posadas*[7] and how the wise men went from house to house, searching for the Christ child.

His paper was rejected because he mentioned the name of Jesus in the second paragraph. Since baby Jesus was the object of the wise men's search, it was impossible to tell the story without including His name. But under the rationale that church and state must be separated, his paper was rejected.

Well, this father was at the school in short order. After a brisk conversation with the teacher and the principal and an absolute promise that a lawsuit would follow if that paper was not accepted, common sense suddenly prevailed. But unfortunately, this hostile environment toward Christianity continues to grow in far too many American public schools.

Recently a school principal in Jackson, Mississippi, allowed a student to read this prayer over the public address system: "Almighty God, we ask Your blessing on our teachers, our parents, and our nation. Amen."

The result? The principal was immediately put on probation and forced to call in by phone every hour and report his activities to authorities. Criminals on parole are treated better.

Today in most American public schools you can distribute condoms, teach lifeboat ethics, and affirm that it's normal for Heather to have "two [lesbian] mommies," but you can't read the Bible. What would John Quincy Adams have said in response to this? One of our nation's founding fathers, he declared, "So great is my veneration for the Bible that the earlier my children begin to read it, the more confident will be my hope that they will prove useful citizens for their country and respectable members of society. I have for many years made it a practice to read the Bible through once every year."[8] Today Quincy would be despised as a bigot and arrested as a law-breaker, as would Abraham Lincoln for having the audacity to say, "I believe the Bible is the best gift God has given to man."[9]

And yet the Supreme Court has ruled that it is unconstitutional for the Ten Commandments to be posted on a classroom wall. Why? Because students might read them and the words might affect their moral character. Heaven help us, for in a generation marked by drive-by shootings, murder, rape, teenage suicides, drug abuse, homosexuality, pornography, and satanism, we certainly wouldn't want to affect moral character development! "Political correctness" is the new commandment foisted on all children.

What irony! Russia, formerly an atheistic state, is desperately trying to repair the moral wreckage brought upon its people by godlessness. Immediately after the collapse of the Soviet regime, the people were begging for Bibles, for copies of the Ten Commandments, for preachers and ministry groups to participate in their public school programs. Yet in America, one of the most "religious" countries on earth, we forbid those very things!

For thirty years the minds of our children have been vacuumed and sanitized. They have been taught political correctness. They know how to put a condom on a banana and why they should be sensitive to spotted owls and sucker fish. But CBS released a poll that stated that 75 percent of America's recent high school graduates can't name the last three presidents of the United States.

An educational commission said of the American public school system, "If a foreign power had done to our schools what we have done, we would consider it an act of war."

Believe me, friends, a new world order is coming and a new world orderer (the Antichrist), but this new world order is not going to be the utopia that politicians, professors, and pundits have predicted. It's going to be hell on earth, a time of severe tribulation and testing. And it will come from Satan's false messiah, the Antichrist, the so-called man of peace who will make Hitler look like a choirboy! He will set himself up as God—and people will believe in him by the millions.

The Antichrist's One World Religion

What is the Antichrist's chief desire? He is a false christ, and Christ is worthy of our worship and praise. Satan knows the prophecy that one day every knee will bow before Jesus Christ, but so great is his hatred toward God that he's determined to lash out at God by keeping as many people from salvation as possible. And who knows, maybe Satan even thinks he can defeat the Lord God somehow. During the Antichrist's limited time on earth, he wants to be worshiped. He will set up his image in Jerusalem and all who refuse to worship him will be murdered (see Rev. 13:15).

Jesus confirmed that Satan's messiah, the Antichrist, will demand worldwide worship. "'Therefore when you see the "abomination of desolation," spoken of by Daniel the prophet, standing in the holy place' (whoever reads, let him understand), 'then let those who are in Judea flee to the mountains'" (Matt. 24:15).

The Jewish temple will be rebuilt in Jerusalem. During the first half of his rule, the Antichrist will allow the Jewish people to resume making sacrifices in the temple. They will rejoice and many of them may even believe him to be their Messiah. But during the last three-and-a-half years of his reign, he will forbid the offering of sacrifices.

The last time I was in Israel, I was amazed to discover that a temple society there has already made all of the implements necessary for temple worship to be reinstated exactly as in the days of Moses. Every detail in every instrument and every fabric has been replicated as they prepare to make daily sacrifices in the temple again.

Daniel makes it clear that the continual burnt offering stops three-and-a-half years (1,290 days) before the end of the Tribulation. Why? The Antichrist will introduce idolatrous worship inside the holy temple and set himself up as God: "He will confirm a covenant with many for one 'seven,' [a term of seven years] but in the middle of that 'seven' he will put an end to sacrifice and offering. And one who causes desolation will place abominations on a wing of the temple until the end that is decreed is poured out on him" (Dan. 9:27 NIV).

"He opposes and exalts himself over everything that is called God or is worshiped, and even sets himself up in God's temple, proclaiming himself to be God" (2 Thess. 2:4 NIV). The Antichrist is not alone. In this perverted satanic trinity, Satan (the first person of this twisted trinity) supplies the power to the Antichrist (the second person), who in turn has a helper, the devilish "False Prophet," who works signs and wonders in the Antichrist's name (just as the Holy Spirit does in the Blessed Trinity): "And he [the False Prophet] deceives those who dwell on the earth by those signs which he was granted to do in the sight of the beast, telling those who dwell on the earth to make an image to the beast who was wounded by the sword and lived. He was granted power to give breath to the image of the beast, that the image of the beast should both speak and cause as many as would not worship the image of the beast to be killed" (Rev. 13:14–15). Through the False Prophet's demonic power, the image of the Antichrist is made to speak like a man.

The False Prophet is to the Antichrist what the Holy Spirit is to Jesus Christ. When the False Prophet causes this statue to speak, most will bow and worship on the spot.

The fact that the Antichrist will present himself to the world as God is verified in Daniel 11:36: "Then the king [Antichrist] shall do according to his own will: he shall exalt and magnify himself above every god, shall speak blasphemies against the God of gods, and shall prosper till the wrath has been accomplished; for what has been determined shall be done."

Israel has yet to endure her darkest night. I believe the peace process now under way will prove alas to be a Trojan horse. Instead of bringing the long-sought-for peace, it will bring the Antichrist and the most horrible war the Holy Land has ever known. The religious Jews of Israel are about to experience the most blasphemous campaign of all time to force them to abandon their faith when the Antichrist demands that they worship his image in the holy city of Jerusalem or else.

CHAPTER EIGHT

Conspiracies, Coalitions, and Catastrophies

A "man of peace" quite different from Yitzhak Rabin will soon step onto the world's stage. One of his foremost Bible names is "the son of perdition" (2 Thess. 2:3), which can also be translated as "chief son of Satan."

The Son of Satan

Time magazine, in its review of the movie *The Omen,* noted that this dark and disturbing movie "rests on the biblical prophecy about the return of the Prince of Darkness taken from *The Revelator* to fit certain events of our time—the creation of Israel and the Common Market [now known as the European Union]."[1] The magazine article concluded that these are "times to believe in a reincarnated devil."

The Antichrist's origin, methods, agenda, and goal are clearly revealed in Bible prophecy. The Antichrist, or deceptive "man of peace," could very well be alive right now.

The Strategy of Satan

But in order to fully understand the agenda of the Antichrist, it is important to grasp the overall strategy of Satan. Satan's goal is to "be like the Most High" (Is. 14:14). In fact, he wants to go beyond that and *dethrone* the Most High.

Somewhere in the early dawn of time, Satan, the most perfect being ever created, convinced one-third of the angels to join him in his reckless attempt to supplant God as the ruler of all. Decisively defeated, Satan has continued in open opposition to God, seeking wherever possible to lash out at God and to attempt to destroy, deceive, or discredit that which is important to Him.

We get a hint of this from the very name "antichrist." The prefix *anti-* in Greek has two meanings. The first is what we naturally think of in English: against. The second is in some ways far more interesting, for *anti-* also means "in place of." And both of these definitions apply in the case of the Antichrist: Satan and his unholy conspirators are both against God and seeking to take the place of God.

Certainly Satan and his demons know what the Word of God says about their ultimate doom, so why do they persist in this ultimately futile endeavor? There is no doubt that part of the answer could lie in the evil and spite that are the defining qualities of their character. It could also be because somehow Satan and his demons fancy that they can alter their destiny and actually dethrone God Almighty. After all, Satan's original sin was pride. Certainly evil is at the very core of Satan's motivation, but I believe the very events of the Tribulation demonstrate that Satan still believes he can ultimately succeed in taking God's place, and that is why Satan's works in the Tribulation so doggedly and yet so ineffectively attempt to imitate the worldwide rule of God in the Millennium.

With "the Restrainer" (the Holy Spirit at work on the earth through the Church) removed, Satan feels he has the best shot he has ever had in taking God's place. But what Satan has in the way of opportunity, he lacks in the realm of originality.

Just as the One God has existed for all eternity as Father, Son, and Holy Spirit, so Satan creates his own twisted trinity of Satan, the Antichrist, and the False Prophet.

But while the Father omnipotent rules from heaven on high, Satan is cast down from heaven and confined first to a bottomless pit and then to hell, the eternal lake of fire.

While Jesus offers eternal salvation to those who will trust Him, the Antichrist can only provide eternal damnation for those foolish enough to trust him. And while Jesus will rule a world of peace and prosperity during the thousand-year period known as the Millennium, the Antichrist will rule (if you can call it ruling) for a mere seven years—years which are characterized by unprecedented war, deprivation, and chaos.

While the Holy Spirit testifies of Jesus and provides comfort, joy, and strength to those who follow the Savior, the False Prophet testifies of the Antichrist and enforces allegiance to him through threats, deception, and naked aggression.

Satan knows that God is planning a thousand-year rule over the earth—one thousand years that will be characterized by one world religion, one world government, one world economy. So of course Satan tries to implement the same thing.

Satan seeks to impose one world religion, but instead "a great multitude that no one can count" rejects this religion and recognizes Jesus as their Messiah. And while Jesus offers eternal salvation to those who trust Him, the Antichrist can only promise temporal salvation (the ability to buy and sell) to those who deny Christ.

Satan seeks to impose a single world government, but instead the Antichrist seems to spend at least the second half of the Tribulation fighting off one challenge after another to his rule—only to have his one-world government of one thousand years cut short at seven.

Satan seeks worldwide compliance to his laws, but the best the Antichrist can do is to rush around attempting to quash one rebellion after another. And he will never fully succeed.

The Number of a Man: 666

John the Revelator writes, "Here is wisdom. Let him who has understanding calculate the number of the beast, for it is the number of a man [or, the number of man]: His number is 666" (Rev. 13:18). The meaning of the number "666" provides an ideal transition from looking at the satanic trinity as a whole to focusing on the second member of that Trinity, the Antichrist.

"The number of a man," according to Bible scholars, is six. Under the Law, man's labor was limited to six days, for God created man to rest on the seventh day. The seventh day is God's day, and seven is the number of divine completeness throughout the Scripture. Six falls short of seven, just as anything done by created beings falls short of the Creator's perfection.

The Antichrist's number of 666 could also represent the satanic trinity: Satan, the Antichrist, and the False Prophet who will lead the worldwide cult that worships the son of Satan. For just as six falls short of seven, we have seen that Satan falls short of being God the Father, the Antichrist falls short of being God the Son, and the False Prophet falls short of being God the Holy Spirit.

The number 666 could also be a reference to the worldwide idolatry attempted by Nebuchadnezzar when he erected a statue of himself and commanded all the world to worship it or face death (see Dan. 3). You might say that 666 was stamped upon the very image of Nebuchadnezzar since the image was 60 cubits high and 6 cubits wide (see v. 1).

Now remember, in Revelation 13 the focal point is the rise of a man, the Antichrist, and 666 is said to be "the number of a man." In light of this emphasis, there is another possible explanation of the cryptic name "666." I am speculating here, but certainly some of John's readers were familiar with method of calculating a name by the use of numbers, a practice known to the Jews as *Geometria* (or *Gimetria*). The Greeks also practiced it, but not as seriously as the Jewish people.

This transition from number to letter or from letter to number was possible because most ancient languages did not have independent symbols for numbers as we do. Rather, the letters of the alphabet were also used to designate numbers in the way that Roman numerals use letters to designate numbers. It was a simple matter for members of the early church to convert a number into a name or a name into a number.

In Revelation 13:18 John made it possible for the world to identify the Antichrist. This cryptic puzzle is not intended to point a finger at some unknown person. It is, however, intended to confirm to the world someone already suspected as being the Antichrist. And in the idolatry of the end time, "the number of a man" is fully developed and the result is 666.

This information about how to identify the Antichrist is of no practical value to the Church since we will be watching from the balconies of heaven by the time he is revealed. But for those of you who are reading this book after the church has been taken in the Rapture, and for those of you who come to trust Christ during the Tribulation, you will have the ability to confirm which personality rising out of a European federation is the devil incarnate, the son of Satan.

During the late 1930s and early 1940s a flurry of pamphlets identified Adolf Hitler as the Antichrist. Others declared that Mussolini was the Antichrist because of his relationship to Rome. But no one who lives from the time of Pentecost until the Rapture of the church can possibly know who the Antichrist is because he will not make his appearance upon the world stage until the Church, indwelt by the Restrainer, the Holy Spirit, has been removed from the earth.

This so-called man of peace, this son of Satan, this false messiah, the Antichrist, is probably alive right now and may even know his predestined demonic assignment. And though we may not know who the Antichrist *is,* we certainly know in great detail what the Antichrist will *do.*

The Antichrist Described

In the thirteenth chapter of Revelation we find one of the most descriptive accounts of the Antichrist's activities. Here he is referred to as "the Beast," whose number is 666. In Daniel, where he is described even more fully, you will recall that he is the "little horn" of chapter seven. He is also referred to as the "king of fierce features" of Daniel 8, the "prince who is to come" in chapter nine, and the "willful king" of chapter eleven.

As we have already shown, the son of Satan will be a counterfeit of the son of God. But we learn even more about the personality and plan of the Antichrist by understanding how completely opposite he is from Jesus, the true Son of God.

Christ came from heaven (John 6:38)	the Antichrist will come from hell (Rev. 11:7)
Christ came in His Father's name (John 5:43)	the Antichrist will come in his own name (John 5:43)
Christ humbled Himself (Phil. 2:8)	the Antichrist will exalt himself (2 Thess. 2:4)
Christ was despised and afflicted (Is. 53:3)	the Antichrist will be admired and lauded (Rev. 13:3, 4)
Christ came to do His Father's will (John 6:38)	the Antichrist will come to do his own will (Dan. 11:36)
Christ came to save (Luke 19:10)	the Antichrist will come to destroy (Dan. 8:24)
Christ is the Good Shepherd (John 10)	the Antichrist will be the Evil Shepherd (Zech. 11:16, 17)
Christ is the Truth (John 14:6)	the Antichrist will be "the lie" (2 Thess. 2:11)
Christ is the Mystery of Godliness, God manifested in the flesh (1 Tim. 3:16)	the Antichrist will be "The Mystery of Iniquity," Satan manifested in the flesh (2 Thess. 2:7–9), the living son of Satan

The Antichrist Comes to Power

The Antichrist will first take control of one nation in the federated block, which could come from the current European Union. At a moment of instability, which could be caused by war in Bosnia or some United Nations sanctioned action, he will take control of three nations within the federation:

John describes him in Revelation 13:1: "Then I stood on the sand of the sea. And I saw a beast rising up out of the sea, having seven heads and ten horns, and on his horns ten crowns, and on his heads a blasphemous name."

Notice that the beast rises from the sea—the sea, in prophetic symbolism, represents the Gentile world—and he wears ten crowns on seven heads. In other words, he has conquered three of ten nations and rules over them, wearing ten symbolic crowns.

Israel Entrusts Its Security to the Antichrist

Desperate for peace and ignorant of the Antichrist's true nature, Israel will soon sign a seven-year treaty of peace with the Antichrist. In fact, the signing of the treaty is the event that will inaugurate the seven-year Tribulation. In this treaty the Antichrist himself will guarantee Israel's security. "He [the Antichrist] will confirm a covenant with many for one 'seven.' In the middle of that 'seven' he will put an end to sacrifice and offering" (Dan. 9:27 NIV).

Now before reading on, just take a moment to think about what the Word of God says. If you've ever been to Israel, you'll note that their history of betrayal and persecution makes them extremely wary to entrust their safety to anyone other than themselves. In fact, this history is part of the great need for the Jewish people to have their own homeland—they can trust their government because their government is truly their own. You could even say that the nation of Israel is an incarnation of their desire as expressed in the solemn utterance "Never again." Never again a pogrom; never again a persecution; never again an exile; never again a holocaust. So just imagine what it would take for them to entrust their security to another. This gives you an idea both of the coming change of attitude in Israel and of the incredible power and credibility of the Antichrist.

In the months ahead, it is a distinct possibility—and as far as I'm concerned a probability—that Israel will relinquish all or part of the Golan Heights to Syria and then invite the United Nations or some other international force to occupy that region to guarantee their national security. That will be a defining moment in history because the nation of Israel has never relied upon anyone else for its national safety.

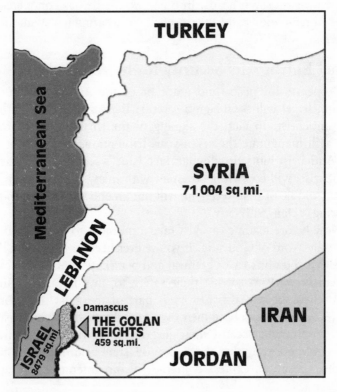

The Golan Heights, a strategic plateau overlooking northern Israel and the southern Syrian plains, is critical both militarily and as the principal source of water for the nation of Israel. The area is a towering plateau about twelve miles wide that measures about 480 square miles and is distinguished by two levels; the Lower Golan in the south, with altitudes between 600 and 1,900 feet, and the Upper Golan in the north, rising to altitudes of up to 3,000 feet above sea level. A number of hilltops reach as high as 4,400 feet.

The Israeli observation posts on the Golan Heights make it virtually impossible for Syria to launch a sneak attack against Israel, and weather conditions are such that satellite surveillance would be difficult and airborne surveillance extremely costly.

As a small country, Israel has no land that can be yielded to an attacker during the first blow of a military attack. Accordingly the IDF (Israel Defense Forces) have always relied heavily on preemptive strikes and rapid mobilization of reserves to resist hostile enemies massed on their borders. But this also means that it is an absolute necessity for Israel to have accurate and timely information to anticipate and preempt any military actions by their enemies.

And while it is true that the Syrians can reach any location in Israel from any location in Syria with their Scud-C missiles (whether the missiles carry conventional or chemical warheads), it is also true that the Golan Heights is laid out in such a way that a Syrian invasion can only come through two areas: the Tel Fars area and the Quneitra area. This explains why when the Israelis were completely surprised by the Yom Kippur war and initially overrun by Egypt, a small force of heroic Israeli troops were able to hold at bay one thousand Syrian tanks until the reserves were able to reach the area. However, had the Israelis not had the Golan Heights, they would have had to repel an attack inside Israel in the heavily populated Hula Valley, the Jordan Valley, and the Galilee. The casualties would have been horrific.

Perhaps even more important on a day-to-day basis, the Golan Heights are rich in water resources, and these resources are in desperate demand in the desert that comprises so much of Israel and the Middle East. By contrast, Syria is rich in water resources and has regularly tried to dry out Israel by diverting the sources of the Jordan River.[2]

Since June 1974, as many as 1,250 troops of the United Nations Disengagement Observer Force have patrolled the area of separation between Israeli and Syrian forces. Obviously there aren't enough of them to prevent aggression because of their limited size and strength. Instead they are "trip wires"— like the allied forces were in West Berlin during the Cold War. Our forces could have been overwhelmed by the Communists, but to do so they would have had to take the lives of allied soldiers, and thus make *full* allied involvement in a *wider* war *inevitable*. So the UN troops are human shields and hostages, ensuring that the aggressor who harms them will face the wrath of the world community.[3] Nevertheless, right now it can be said that only in some small ways is the UN acting as a guarantor of peace for Israel. Yet far from entrusting their security to the UN, the IDF actively and vigorously maintains a defense of the Golan, and it maintains the fourth most powerful military force in the world.

Yet outrage at the assassination of Prime Minister Yitzhak Rabin will unite Israeli public opinion and galvanize their government to pursue peace with the Palestinians and Syrians. Just a few months ago, world leaders and theologians would have considered this utterly impossible, but it is happening now before our very eyes.

Rabin believed in peace strongly enough to stake the final portion of his political career—and ultimately, his life—in persuit of it. Now the world watches to see who will lead the country after the next election. But since Leah Rabin has publicly blamed Binyamin Netanyahu for her husband's murder, it is likely that Shimon Peres, the current Prime Minister, will lead Israel in the months ahead. By law, Peres will have up to forty-two days—two twenty-one-day periods—to form a government and have it approved by a majority of the one-hundred-twenty-member Knesset.[4]

According to experts in Israeli politics, before the Rabin assassination "the truism of Israel politics was: Peres was too eager to shake Arafat's hand, while Rabin was just reluctant enough to do it."[5] But now the world is eager for the Israelis to shake the Arabs' hands. Shimon Peres, often described as "the dovish foreign minister," was the chief negotiator with the Palestinians. He initiated the secret contacts in Oslo, Norway, that led to the 1993 West Bank Accord.

So despite Israel's history, the transition to a less defensive posture is already underway. When the time comes, so great will be the confidence and trust of the Israelis in the protection of the Antichrist that when they are attacked just before the three-and-a-half-year mark of the Tribulation, they will be described as "a land of unwalled villages . . . a peaceful people, who dwell safely, all of them dwelling without walls, and having neither bars nor gates" (Ez. 38:11). Now this is absolutely remarkable. If you've ever been to Israel, you know that security is their top priority—soldiers, machine guns, tanks, walls, and concertina wire are everywhere! It would be one thing if you found a prophetic reference to a tranquil nation like Costa Rica that is free of defenses, but it's something else altogether for a nation like Israel to surrender its national security to a foreign military force.

Perhaps it is because of the euphoria they will feel over the rebuilding of the Temple.

The Temple Is Rebuilt

One of the specifications of the agreement between Israel and the Antichrist will allow the religious Jews to rebuild the Temple and to initiate daily sacrifices. We know this because the Antichrist will stop sacrifices and offerings at the mid-point of the Tribulation, and sacrifices have to have been started again in order for the Antichrist to stop them. Another clue that the Temple will be rebuilt is that the Antichrist will take over the Temple, an event which also occurs at the midpoint of the Tribulation: "He [the Antichrist] opposes and exalts himself over everything that is called God or is worshiped, and even sets himself up in God's temple, proclaiming himself to be God" (2 Thess. 2:4). Again, a temple must have been built in order for the Antichrist to seize and defile it as he will.

Now the rebuilding of the Temple constitutes an enormous political and religious problem, for the place the Bible decrees for the location of the Temple is currently occupied by the Dome of the Rock.

The Dome of the Rock, located on the temple mount, or Mount Moriah, is the third holiest place in the world for Muslims. Listen to it described by The Islamic Association for Palestine:

> "Glory be to Him Who did take His servant for a journey by night from the sacred (Haram) mosque to the farthest (Aqsa) mosque whose precincts We did bless, in order that We might show him some of Our signs: for He is the One Who hears and sees (all things)" (Qur'an 17:1). Al-Aqsa mosque is the third holiest place in Islam, the second house of worship on Earth, and was the first direction of prayer for Muslims. One prayer in Al-Aqsa mosque is equivalent to 500 times the prayers in any other mosque except for the Haram Mosque in Makka and the Prophet's (An-Nabawi) Mosque in Madina. In the journey to heaven, Prophet Muhammed (pbuh) prayed in Al-Aqsa mosque, leading all the prophets.[6]

If you doubt that the Jewish people would ever attempt something so audacious, you need to know that some Jewish people are *already* planning for it, working to make all the necessary preparations for the construction and operation of the *third* Temple (the first being Solomon's and the second being Herod's). One of the organizations working toward this end is called the Temple Foundation. Here is how they describe their work:

> Today, at the Temple Institute in Jerusalem, Biblical prophecy is being fulfilled. Here, you can see something which has not been seen on the face of the earth for 2,000 years: In preparation for the Third Temple, the Temple Institute has created authentic Temple vessels and priestly garments according to Biblical specifications. This is an ongoing process, and to date over 60 sacred objects have been recreated from gold, silver and copper. These vessels are not models or replicas, but they are actually made according to all the complicated nuances and requirements of Biblical law. If the Holy Temple were to be rebuilt immediately, the Divine service could be resumed utilizing these vessels. . . .
>
> In addition to its work on the recreation of Temple vessels, the Institute is conducting a number of related research projects. These include the importation of authentic Red Heifers to Israel, in preparation for the ritual purification detailed in Numbers 19. Other firsts include the identification and gathering together of all 11 ingredients of the incense offering, and the long and exhaustive research in identifying the stones of the High Priest's breastplate—the Urim and Thummim. There is even advanced work being done by technicians and architects, using sophisticated computer technology, to design actual blueprints for the Third Temple.[7]

Only the destruction of the great mosques in Mecca and Medina could have a more explosive effect on Muslims. And perhaps no greater blow (apart from the battles described in this chapter and the next) has ever been inflicted on them than what Israel will accomplish in the removal of the Dome of the Rock to build the third Temple. But even as an international force guarantees the security of Israel in their decision to rebuild the Temple, the Islamic nations will prepare for war. The "King of the North" will lead them toward Israel.

An Islamic Jihad Against Israel

In response to the destruction of the Dome of the Rock, the Islamic nations of Africa and the Middle East will form a Pan-Islamic Coalition to destroy Israel, eliminate the Jewish people, and destroy the third Temple. Of course the removal of the Dome of the Rock in and of itself will seem like reason enough for the Islamic nations of Africa and the Middle East to put aside their historic and multifaceted squabbles. Yet building this alliance will take time, and the Coalition will not strike until around the middle of the seven-year Tribulation. Yet I believe that Israel, while enjoying a time of relative peace, will nevertheless be continuously hounded by terrorist groups like HAMAS and the Islamic Jihad.

But we must also remember that militant Islam harbors so much hatred toward the Jewish people that it won't take much to work them into a frenzy to accomplish what they have longed for for years: "Six million descendents of monkeys [i.e., Jews] now rule all the nations of the world, but their day, too, will come. Allah, Kill them all, do not leave even one."[8]

The Scriptures describe this coming Coalition as a confederation of two great kings: the King of the South and the King of the North.

The King of the South, according to Ezekiel, will control the borders that were then known as Persia, Ethiopia, and Libya. Persia is modern-day Iran, the present incubator and disseminator of militant Islam. Libya here (literally "Put"), refers to the same general area that the modern terrorist state of Libya now occupies. Ethiopia may represent more than the one country that now bears its name. Its ancestry is traced to Cush, a grandson of Noah (see Genesis 10), whose descendants must have migrated southward into all parts of Africa.

Nothing could make more sense in the light of current events. The Islam of the Iranian fundamentalists is on the march in Africa, not only in north Africa but throughout the entire continent as well. Right now, there is an epic battle raging between Christianity and Islam for the hearts and souls of men and women in Africa. With the church removed from that continent, Islam will have an open road to proselytize. And interestingly, The Islamic Association for Palestine reports:

- That the original 1947 recommendation to create a "Jewish State" in Palestine was approved, at the first vote, only by European, American, and Australian States . . . for every Asian State, and every African State (with the exception of the Union of South Africa) voted against it.

- That, when the vote was cast in plenary session on 29 November 1947, urgent American pressures (which a member of the Truman cabinet described as "bordering onto scandal") had succeeded in prevailing only upon one African country (Liberia) . . . which had special vulnerability to American pressures, to abandon their declared opposition.

- That Israel remained, ever since its inception, a total stranger in the emerging world of Afro-Asia; and that Israel has been refused admission to any inter-state conference of Asian, African, Afro-Asian, or Non-Aligned States ever held.[9]

Now if even half of those statements are true, it is clear that there will be no shortage of volunteers from Africa to take up arms against Israel (to say nothing of her enemies in the Middle East).

Also mentioned as conspiring with the Coalition of the Kings of the South and North are the nations of Sheba (modern Yeman), Dedan (a territory in Southern Edom, located today in southern Jordan), and Tarshish (which is traditionally identified as being on the coast of southern Spain or the Mediterranean island of Sardinia).

The other dread participant in this coming Jihad is the King of the North. Looking at the modern location of the names of the combatants mentioned in Ezekiel 38 and 39 and their location as shown on the map entitled "The Nations of Genesis 10," it becomes clear that they come from the general area of Turkey, Syria, Iraq, and at least some of the Islamic republics of the former (and I believe future) Soviet Union, if not from Russia herself.[10]

Don't count Russia out of this coming Jihad that will take place just before the halfway point of the Tribulation. In Ezekiel 38 and 39 there are tantalizing references to "Gog, of the land of Magog" (38:2) who "will come from [his] place out of the far north, [he] and many peoples [or nations] with [him], all of them riding on horses, a great company and a mighty army" (Ez. 38:15). And while no one knows the exact

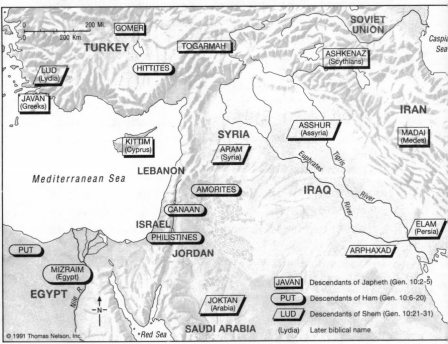

The Nations of Genesis 10

location of the land of Magog, going north from Israel will eventually land you in Russia. And even if it is later determined that the land of Magog is located in modern-day Turkey or the land bridge between the Black and Caspian Seas,[11] this does not rule out the possibility that these areas are conquered by Russia in the days immediately before the Rapture (which I believe we are living in) or immediately after.

Whatever the identity of "Gog, of the land of Magog," it is leading many nations in the war against Israel and the Jewish people. Interestingly enough, a substantial number of the nations mentioned in Ezekiel 38 and 39 have been allied with Russia in recent times: "These include Iran ('Persia'), Sudan and northern Ethiopia ('Cush'), Libya ('Put'), and Turkey ('Meshesh,' 'Tubal,' 'Gomer,' and 'Beth Togarmah')."[12]

A Reborn Russia Conspires with Islam

You may be asking, "How could the Soviet Union ever be reborn?" or, "What interest would either Russia or a reborn Soviet Union have in cooperating in this military campaign against Israel and the temple in Jerusalem?" or for that matter, "Why would this Muslim Coalition have any interest in teaming up with Russia?" The answer is as close as today's newspaper.

Russia's Motivation

Now make no mistake, this alliance will be a marriage of convenience—not love. Each will have something that the other wants. For Russia, two things stand out.

Russia longs to be a superpower again. The empire the Soviets built during the time of Communist rule was a source of great pride to many. The humiliation of losing that empire combined with the impoverishment of their faltering economy have left the Russian people romantic about their past, bitter about their present, and skeptical about their future. It is in such a climate that dictatorship grows, and indeed you need look no further than the recent elections to the Russian Duma to find an indication of where Russia is headed. While the leading politicians of Russia are separated on many issues, Gennadi Zyuganov, the leader of the resurgent Communist Party; Vladimir Zhirinovsky, the deranged ultranationalist; and Aleksandr Lebed, the former general are all looking at the future through the lens of their authoritarian and atheist past. They are relying on the resentment of the Russian people toward reform and the West to sweep them into office. And once in office, they must deliver.

As it now stands, the Russian constitution vests far more powers in the president than in the parliament. And because the top two vote-getters in the presidential election face a runoff with each other, the system greatly favors coalition governments. And indeed the process of forming coalitions to reverse the reforms of Gorbachev and Yeltsin has already begun.[13]

Russia has much natural wealth, but it is hard to access. Not only does Russia long to be a superpower again, she also needs money. Unfortunately for the world, when a nation combines poverty with ambition the result is almost always an effort to expand. For while Russia longs for the glory days, right now it has trouble even paying its armed forces. And although Russia is rich with oil reserves and other natural resources, those riches tend to be located in remote areas that are difficult to access. This problem is compounded by their rudimentary technology and their lack of hard currency to buy technology from the West. And after being defeated in Afghanistan and bloodied in Chechnya, Russia's nationalist leaders may believe that the country needs a military victory to increase their prestige and send a suitable message to the world—especially the West.

So to regain its empire, Russia needs money, military victory, and western technology—but on Russia's terms, not by going hat in hand to the West. What better way to achieve all three than by controlling the main source of the industrialized world's oil—the Persian Gulf? By controlling and selling Middle Eastern oil, Russia would be able to blackmail the industrialized nations into submission.

If the Islamic nations cede some control of their oil to Russia in return for her cooperation in the invasion, then the price will be right for her to join the Islamic nations in their campaign to destroy Israel and the temple.

What the Islamic Coalition Gains

What could the Islamic nations possibly get from Russia that would be worth allowing the Russians into their land and giving them control over their oil riches? I can think of at least four reasons.

The Islamic nations would greatly benefit from the strength of Russia's armed forces. Although they are much less powerful than they were during the Cold War, Russia's armed forces are vastly superior to those of any of the Muslim countries, and provide them with a formidable threat in both land, sea, air, and space. Furthermore, the Islamic countries will be only too aware of their inability to defeat Israel's military and the considerable military prowess of the Antichrist, who is guaranteeing the security of Israel.

Russia will be able to threaten to use its nuclear, biological, or chemical weapons, should either Israel or the West threaten to intervene or escalate the conflict by using such weapons. It has long been known that Israel possesses nuclear weapons, as I talked about in a previous chapter, and we can only assume that it has chemical and biological weapons as well to be able to respond to any attack or threat in kind.

Now it is unclear from Ezekiel 38:11 if Israel has retained its arsenal, but even if it has, the Russians can threaten to lob missiles loaded with nuclear, chemical, or biological warheads upon Israel from the relative safety of their borders in the far north, should Israel try to escalate the conflict.

But perhaps even more significant, Russia can threaten the Antichrist with its arsenal, should he try to fulfill his treaty obligations and come to the defense of Israel. And as enraged as the Muslims are about the rebuilding of the Temple and the very existence of Israel, ceding a measure of control over their oil might seem a reasonable price for ridding the world fully and finally of the Jewish State.

Many of the nations identified in Ezekiel 38 and 39 have been past allies of the Russians. Returning to a former alliance may give them a feeling of familiarity, security, and even control.

The Islamic nations may be mindful of Russia's experience in Afghanistan. Remember, as I said earlier, Islam is a religion of truimphalism. It believes that time and history are on its side. So even if eventually their alliance with Russia ruptures and they find themselves at war with her, they may very well believe that they will ultimately prevail over Russia, as was the case in the Afghanistan war.

Why Israel?

As I'm sure you can guess, there are two primary reasons to focus on the elimination of Israel: its religious importance and its strategic importance.

For the Islamic nations, the erection of the third temple on Mount Moriah and the elimination of their Dome of the Rock will be an affront so profound and disturbing that they simply must respond. To get an idea of the depth of their anger, if you're Jewish, imagine what you feel when you see a Nazi propaganda film and multiply that emotion by ten. If you're Christian, imagine what you feel when you hear that an exhibition of art featuring a crucifix submerged in a beaker of urine was paid for through the tax dollars provided to the National Endowment for the Arts; again, multiply that anger and indignation by ten. Even at that, your feeling will not compare with depth of feeling the Muslims will have over the elimination of the Dome of the Rock and the construction of the third temple on its former site. This combined with their deep-seated hatred of the Jewish people will be more than enough to spur them to spend anything and sacrifice anything to eliminate the object of their abhorrence.

Of more importance to the Russians will be Israel's strategic importance. In order to control the oil of the Middle East, in order to dictate peace to the Antichrist on its own terms, Israel must be eliminated as a threat. By guaranteeing the peace of Israel, the Antichrist establishes a friendly outpost in the very heart of the Muslim world. Thus Israel becomes a forward station in the quest for empire. It will not escape the attention of the Russians that the Antichrist is every bit as determined as she is to build an empire and that some day their empires will clash. Nor will it escape the attention of the Muslims that the religion embraced and propagated by the Antichrist is vastly different from their own (though the religions of both will reject the Divine Trinity and the need of all people to trust Jesus Christ, the Son of God as their Savior and Lord).

Although Israel has no oil, she is poised to control the export of oil from the Middle East. Because of her location and military strength—particularly her air force, if she retains it after entering into the covenant of peace with the Anti-christ—she can disrupt the oil shipping routes in the Eastern Mediterranean, the Suez Canal, the Persian Gulf, and even the Strait of Hormuz. Thus Israel's air force and arsenal give her a trump card over the Muslim's expectation of triumph and the Russians' need to control the oil of the Middle East.

For all of these reasons and more, both the Russians and the Muslims will agree that Israel and the Jewish people must disappear from the Middle East. And just before the midpoint of the Tribulation, they seize their opportunity and attack.

The Battle for Israel and Jerusalem (Ezekiel 38 & 39)

Like so many things, what man intends for evil God intends for good, and this monumental battle between Israel and the coalition of Islam and Russia is no exception. For while this dread army believes that they have devised this battle of their own accord to serve their own ends, in fact it is God the Father who has brought them.

The Kings of the North and South Are Drawn into Battle

Ezekiel 38:4–6 declares:

> I will turn you around, put hooks into your jaws, and lead you out, with all your army, horses, and horsemen, all splendidly clothed, a great company with bucklers and shields, all of them handling swords. Persia, Ethiopia, and Libya are with them, all of them with shield and helmet; Gomer and all its troops; the house of Togarmah from the far north and all its troops—many people are with you.

And again we see the Lord orchestrating the battle in 38:16: "It will be in the latter days that *I* will bring you against My land" (emphasis added).

Instead the Kings of the North and the South only see Israel as "the land of those brought back from the sword and gathered from many people on the mountains of Israel, which had long been desolate; they were brought out of the nations, and now all of them dwell safely" (38:8). As a result of Israel's covenant of peace with the Antichrist and the coalition's own strategic preparations, Israel will appear to be more vulnerable than ever—a "land of unwalled villages . . . a peaceful people, who dwell safely, all of them dwelling without walls, and having neither bars nor gates . . . and against a people gathered from the nations, who have acquired livestock and goods, who dwell in the midst of the land" (38:11, 12).

As a result, the Coalition will "come from [its] place out of the far north, [it] and many peoples with [it], all of them riding on horses, a great company and a mighty army. [The coalition] will come up against My people Israel like a cloud, to cover the land" (38:15, 16).

And yet in spite of their strength and initial occupation of the land, the defeat of the Russian-Islamic coalition will be sudden, horrible, and complete.

The Kings of the North and South Are Defeated in Battle

The Kings of the North and South find an easy entry into the Promised Land. As they had hoped, the Antichrist makes no move whatsoever to fulfill his treaty obligations to Israel. And so with gratefulness to Allah (or Lenin), they are about to execute their plan of plunder and genocide. The vast majority will never know what hit them.

The battle is the Lord's. King David identified the source of Israel's military might: "He who keeps Israel shall neither slumber nor sleep" (Ps. 121:4). After watching the Jews of the Holocaust walk into the gas chambers, after seeing the "apple of His eye" thrown into the ovens and their ashes dumped by the tons into the rivers of Europe, after seeing the "land of milk and honey" run red with Jewish blood in five major wars for peace and freedom, God stands up and shouts to the nations of the world, "Enough! My fury shall come up in my face."

God shatters His silence.

"'Surely in that day there shall be a great earthquake in the land of Israel, so that the fish of the sea, the birds of the heavens, the beasts of the field, all creeping things that creep on the earth, and all men who are on the face of the earth shall shake at My presence. The mountains shall be thrown down, the steep places shall fall, and every wall shall fall to the ground.' I will call for a sword against Gog throughout all My mountains," says the Lord GOD. "Every man's sword will be against his brother. And I will bring him to judgment with pestilence and bloodshed; I will rain down on him, on his troops, and on the many peoples who are with him, flooding rain, great hailstones, fire, and brimstone. Thus I will magnify Myself and sanctify Myself, and I will be known in the eyes of many nations. Then they shall know that I am the LORD." (Ez. 38:19–23)

God unleashes His supernatural arsenal against Israel's enemies with lethal results. First, He shakes the earth with a mighty earthquake that will neutralize every tank and every foot soldier instantly. Some will doubtless be buried alive.

Second, God causes mass confusion to come upon every army coming against Israel. Every man turns his sword against his brother. This is exactly what God did when He commanded Gideon to blow the trumpets and break the pitchers. The Philistines became divinely confused and turned their swords on each other. Gideon won a great military victory without one casualty. God will do it again in defense of Israel.

This passage could be interpreted in two ways. First, the "fire and brimstone" may refer to Israel's release of nuclear weapons in a last-ditch attempt to prevent annihilation. The second interpretation is that this event is a repeat of Sodom and Gomorrah. God will blast Israel's enemies into oblivion by raining fire and brimstone from heaven. In either case the results are equally catastrophic.

The victory is complete. Ezekiel's graphic account in chapter 39 makes clear just how thorough and disasterous is the defeat of this Russian-Muslim coalition.

Ezekiel opens chapter 39 by stating: "I am against thee, O Gog." When what is left of the world living in the Tribulation looks at the millions of bloated bodies in the warm Israeli sun, this statement will go down in history as one of the greatest understatements of all time.

In this passage God does not tell us how many died, He tells us how many are left: only a "sixth part" (39:2 KJV). That means that the casualty rate for this battle will be 84 percent, unheard of in modern warfare.

The narrative of the aftermath of the war continues. Ezekiel says that the bloated bodies of the enemies of Israel will be a banquet for buzzards. The beasts of the field will have a feast unlike anything since dogs ate the body of Jezebel.

> "You shall fall on the open field; for I have spoken," says the Lord GOD. "And I will send fire on Magog and on those who live in security in the coastlands. Then they shall know that I am the LORD. So I will make My holy name known in the midst of My people Israel, and I will not let them profane My holy name anymore. . . . It will come to pass in that day that I will give Gog a burial place there in Israel, the valley of those who pass by east of the sea; and it will obstruct travelers, because there they will bury Gog and all his multitude. Therefore they will call it the Valley of Hamon Gog. For seven months the house of Israel will be burying them, in order to cleanse the land. Indeed all the people of the land will be burying, and they will gain renown for it on the day that I am glorified," says the Lord GOD. "They will set apart men regularly employed, with the help of a search party, to pass through the land and bury those bodies remaining on the ground, in order to cleanse it. At the end of seven months they will make a search. The search party will pass through the land; and when anyone sees a man's bone, he shall set up a marker by it, till the buriers have buried it in the Valley of Hamon Gog. The name of the city will also be Hamonah. Thus they shall cleanse the land." (Ez. 39:5–7, 11–16)

The dead bodies of the invaders will be strewn in the fields and mountains of Israel, and the burial detail will take seven months and will involve all the people of Israel. Ezekiel hints very strongly that even tourists will be asked to look for stray bodies to mark the spot for burial details. *Hamon-Gog* is a Hebrew word for "the multitude of Gog," which is to become the name of this vast cemetery for the invaders of Israel.

> "And as for you, son of man, thus says the Lord GOD, 'Speak to every sort of bird and to every beast of the field: "Assemble yourselves and come; gather together from all sides to my sacrificial meal which I am sacrificing for you, a great sacrificial meal on the mountains of Israel, that you may eat flesh and drink blood. You shall eat the flesh of the mighty, drink the blood of the princes of the earth, of rams and lambs, of goats and bulls, all of them fatlings of Bashan. You shall eat fat till you are full, and drink blood till you are drunk, at My sacrificial meal which I am sacrificing for you. You shall be filled at My table with horses and riders, with mighty men and with all the men of war," says the Lord GOD.'" (Ez. 39:17–20)

But not only is there tremendous carnage, the weapons left by these devastated forces provide fuel for Israel for seven years—in other words, beyond the Tribulation and into the Millennium:

> "Then those who dwell in the cities of Israel will go out and set on fire and burn the weapons, both the shields and bucklers, the bows and arrows, the javelins and spears; and they will make fires with them for seven years. They will not take wood from the field nor cut down any from the forests, because they will make fires with the weapons; and they will plunder those who plundered them, and pillage those who pillaged them," says the Lord GOD. (Ezekiel 39:9–10)

Can you imagine burning weapons for seven years? I was in Israel during the "Peace in Galilee War" led by General Ariel Sharon back in the eighties. I personally saw Israeli eighteen-wheel trucks bringing back the spoils of war in a convoy that stretched farther than my eye could see. The trucks, bumper-to-bumper coming out of Lebanon, were carrying maximum loads of war booty back to Israel. These were supplies that had been stored in Lebanon by the Soviet Union and were said to be enough to keep 500,000 men in combat for six months. As great as those spoils were, it was only a matter of days before the Israeli army collected and stored them. But Ezekiel describes a war so vast that it will take seven years to burn the weapons of war.

Israel will derive an unexpected benefit from this. Ezekiel says that the war booty from this massive invasion will provide Israel with fuel for seven years, and because of this the forest will be spared.

It has been my pleasure over the years to plant a tree each time I go to Israel. We have a "Night to Honor Israel" plot in an Israeli forest that we systematically add to each time we visit Israel. I'm glad to know that the invading armies will leave such a massive amount of firewood that "my" trees will survive the war!

The Nations Are Made to Understand Because of the Battle

Why does God allow the nations to make war upon Israel? There is only one answer: for the glory of God. Ezekiel makes it very clear that the world will know that God is God Almighty.

Ezekiel declares: "Thus I will magnify Myself and sanctify Myself, and I will be known in the eyes of many nations. Then they shall know that I am the LORD" (38:23).

The earth is full of so-called gods! Some claim Buddha, others Mohammed, some Satan, some gods of their own making, but who is the Almighty God? When the God of Abraham, Isaac, and Jacob finishes mopping up the enemies of Israel on the mountains of Israel (note that Jerusalem and the cities are saved), there will be no doubt that Jehovah God is the Almighty God.

"It will be in the latter days that I will bring you against My land, so that the nations may know Me, when I am hallowed in you, O Gog, before their eyes" (Ez. 38:16).

Truly the only way we can understand the significance of this incredible defeat is to accept it as an act of God, which is what Ezekiel said it is. It accomplishes the purpose of glorifying God before Israel and the world and, as we shall see, finally beginning the return of the much-chastened Israel to the God of Abraham, Isaac, and Jacob. Ezekiel wants the world to know that God supernaturally neutralizes the enemies of Israel and destroys them that His name might be glorified.

The Jewish People Begin to Turn

A second reason for this great display of God's power is to testify to His beloved Jewish people that He alone is their God. Through their miraculous deliverance the hearts of the Jewish people begin to soften again to the God of Abraham, Isaac, and Jacob:

> "So the house of Israel shall know that I am the LORD their God from that day forward. The Gentiles shall know that the house of Israel went into captivity for their iniquity; because they were unfaithful to Me, therefore I hid My face from them. I gave them into the hand of their enemies, and they all fell by the sword. According to their uncleanness and according to their transgressions I have dealt with them, and hidden My face from them.
>
> Therefore thus says the Lord GOD: Now I will bring back the captives of Jacob, and have mercy on the whole house of Israel; and I will be jealous for My holy name—after they have borne their shame, and all their unfaithfulness in which they were unfaithful to Me, when they dwelt safely in their own land and no one made them afraid. When I have brought them back from the peoples and gathered them out of their enemies' lands, and I am hallowed in them in the sight of many nations, then

they shall know that I am the LORD their God, who sent them into captivity among the nations, but also brought them back to their land, and left none of them captive any longer. And I will not hide My face from them anymore; for I shall have poured out My Spirit on the house of Israel, says the Lord GOD." (Ez. 39:22–29)

Now please note very carefully that the Jewish people at this point have yet to accept Jesus as their Messiah. The Bible is very clear that this will happen at the end of the Tribulation, when the Jewish people who remain living "will look on Me whom they pierced. Yes, they will mourn for Him as one mourns for his only son, and grieve for Him as one grieves for a firstborn" (Zech. 12:10). That is the day, the Scripture declares, when "all Israel will be saved" (Rom. 11:26).

But because of this cataclysmic battle on the soil of the Holy Land, the nation of Israel will abandon its disasterous relationship with the Antichrist and begin turning toward the Most High God.

Now the question is, Where was the Antichrist? Didn't he guarantee the peace and safety of Israel? Yes he did . . .

CHAPTER NINE

Violence,
Vengeance . . .
Vindication

The events I am now about to describe will happen very quickly after the ultimately unsuccessful invasion of the Kings of the North and South. Some of these events will occur in a matter of days, others within a few months. But remember, from the time the Antichrist occupies Israel until his conclusive and cataclysmic defeat at the hands of the Messiah, only three-and-a-half years will elapse. It is during this period that the real forces driving the Antichrist become apparent. But before we document the Antichrist's short and steep slide into "the lake of fire burning with brimstone," don't lose track of his goals throughout the Tribulation:

- A one-world government

- A one-world religion

- A one-world economy

And pay very careful attention to his outcome. As the agent and incarnation of Satan on the earth, the Antichrist will accomplish in the Tribulation exactly what Satan has accomplished throughout history:

- He will lie

- He will rob

- He will kill
- He will destroy
- *He will fail*

And when any of us rejects God's authority in any area of our lives, the outcome is as certain as betting on yesterday's football game:

- We will be deceived
- We will be robbed
- We will be killed
- We will be destroyed
- We will not succeed

Today the media would have you believe that the worst thing that could happen to America would be for the so-called "ayatollahs of the Christian right" to set the moral agenda for this nation. Now about the only thing worse than having the "ayatollahs of the Christian right" set the moral agenda for our nation is *not* having them set the moral agenda. And while the exaltation of God in America has brought unparalleled blessings to our land, there is no greater example of what happens when Jehovah God is abandoned and then banished than the state of the world during the reign of the Antichrist—and there is no better time than right now to let the life-giving, devil-defeating, bondage-breaking presence of Jesus the Messiah reign in your heart, your family, and your community.

The Antichrist: Master of Politics

The Antichrist will sit out the Islamic-Russian war over Israel. Following in Satan's footsteps as "a liar and the father of lies," the Antichrist will break the covenant he has made with the nation of Israel first by failing to come to their aid, and then by taking the land of Israel and its temple for himself.

While the Antichrist's actions are contemptible, they are also very shrewd. Instead of coming to the aid of Israel and thus exposing his military to danger, the Antichrist instead will let the Kings of the North and the South expend their resources on their own campaign against Israel. Israel's defeat at the hands of other armies might make her easier for the Antichrist to occupy. On the other hand, should Israel put up a fight and damage either the King of the North or the King of the South, then these weakened rival kingdoms would be even more susceptible to subjugation by him. So goes the Antichrist's reasoning.

Of course the results of this strategy will exceed his wildest imagination. Not only are these invading nations weakened, but with casualty rates of 84 percent, their capacity to wage war or even defend themselves simply does not exist for the moment. And while the Antichrist may have had some reason to worry about his supply of Middle Eastern oil if the Russian-Islamic Coalition would have succeeded, the facts on the ground after the battle are that Africa and the entire Middle East will be his for the taking with hardly the effort it would have taken before their war with Israel. "Yes," the Antichrist thinks, "life *is* good! This is the right time for the other shoe to drop."

The Antichrist: Master of Religion

After the dramatic weakening of the Kings of the North and the South, the Antichrist decides the time is right to extend his influence and power by executing two of the most daring and reckless gambits ever attempted in human history. His first gambit is to abrogate his covenant with Israel.

The importance of Israel—really Jerusalem and its temple—makes sense only in the light of his second gambit: a lightning-swift coup d'état against the key power behind his rise to power—the planet-wide interlocking system of religion and commerce known (at least from God's perspective) as "BAB-YLON THE GREAT, THE MOTHER OF HARLOTS AND OF THE ABOMINATIONS OF THE EARTH" (Rev. 17:5). As you might imagine, being viewed by God as "Babylon" turns out not to be a good thing.

It is easy to develop the impression that the Antichrist rose to the center of the world's stage strictly by virtue of his military prowess. Now while his military prowess is indeed significant, never forget that he also grows in power by virtue of his ability to cunningly form alliances and just as cunningly break them when doing so is to his advantage.

The rise of the Antichrist is due in no small measure to the patronage he enjoys from this Babylonian system, described for us in Revelation chapters 17 and 18. Scholars disagree on the fine points of the exact meaning and timing of this passage, but there is much that is clear.

The system that John reveals as "Babylon the great" will be the dominant force in the world throughout the first half of the Tribulation. She will rule over the nations of the world as well as over the Antichrist and his European federation, which is signified in the book of Revelation by Babylon sitting on top of first the nations and then specifically the Antichrist and his federation (Rev. 17:1–3). Her influence over the world stems from her complete dominance of two major areas: religion and commerce.

As a religious system, it is *powerful*—dominating the earth (17:1); *perverted*—not only glorifying a false god, but sanctioning wicked living (17:2–4); *persecuting*—"I saw the woman, drunk with the blood of the saints and with the blood of the martyrs of Jesus" (17:6).

I believe that the way is already being paved for this world-wide religious system through the spread of New Age religious beliefs. By this I don't mean people who sleep under pyramids, pray to Gaia, wear custom crystals, hug trees, and listen to John Denver music. I mean the growing convergence of religion and morality around a few central beliefs:

- Every practice must be permitted, for we must not judge anyone.*

- Every belief must be respected, for we must not be bigoted toward anyone.*

- Every form of expression must be allowed, for we must not censor anyone.*

Now the asterisks above are significant because they high-light an important exception to each of these principles. In the Babylonian system, and to some extent even now, each of these statements will end with the words "anyone except Christians." It will be perfectly acceptable to judge Christians, to be preju-diced toward Christians, and to censor Christians. In fact, the world will commend these actions. Thus you can see even today that the stage is being set for people to come together based on their hatred of Christians—which is why during the Tribulation this whorish religion called Babylon will be able to kill Christians by the thousands and advance perversion, yet still be regarded as the quintessential guardian of faith and morality. In at least the first half of the Tribulation, political correctness will be god, and Babylon this religion's high priestess.

The commercial aspects of the Babylonian system are set forth in Revelation 18. Bible scholars disagree about whether Babylon will operate commercially before its subjugation by the Antichrist, or if her commerce will begin after the Anti-christ takes her over, specifically when the False Prophet makes buying and selling possible only for those who have "the mark of the Beast."

In any event, this commercial system will be a source of vast wealth for the kings and merchants who choose to make a pact with Babylon:

> "For all the nations have drunk of the wine of the wrath of her fornication, the kings of the earth have committed fornication with her, and the merchants of the earth have become rich

through the abundance of her luxury." . . . "The kings of the earth who committed fornication and lived luxuriously with her will weep and lament for her, when they see the smoke of her burning" . . . "And the merchants of the earth will weep and mourn over her, for no one buys their merchandise anymore." (Rev. 18:3, 9, 11)

As a religious system, Babylon will dominate the spiritual life of the people on earth; as a commercial system, it will determine the prosperity of the merchants and governments on earth. Therefore, it is the most powerful force on earth—a direct obstacle to the Antichrist's schemes to be the central figure in the religion, economy, and government of the earth. Babylon must go—and it happens so swiftly that those watching are dumbfounded, both at the speed of its demise and the consequent obliteration of their source of riches (see Rev. 18:19).

At the level that the Antichrist is aware of, he accumulates the power he needs to eliminate the Babylonian system through a conspiracy with

"ten kings who have received no kingdom as yet, but they receive authority for one hour as kings with the beast. These are of one mind, and they will give their power and authority to the beast. . . . And the ten horns which you saw on the beast, these will hate the harlot, make her desolate and naked, eat her flesh and burn her with fire." (Rev. 17:12–13, 16)

But what the Antichrist does not realize is that God has sovereignly moved to give him the ability to overthrow the Babylonian system—and that soon it will be the Antichrist's turn to experience a judgment that is swift, total, and dreadful: "For God has put it into their hearts to fulfill His purpose, to be of one mind, and to give their kingdom to the beast, until the words of God are fulfilled" (Rev. 17:17).

Once the Antichrist has eliminated Babylon, he will move with alacrity to fill the void with his own system. His first step is to provide a replacement worldwide religion. This is when the temple in Jerusalem becomes important—and this is when his treaty with Israel is cast aside. "Then he shall confirm a covenant with many for one week; but in the middle of the week he shall bring an end to sacrifice and offering. And on the wing of abominations shall be one who makes desolate, even until the consummation, which is determined, is poured out on the desolate" (Dan. 9:27).

The Antichrist not only ignores his own treaty with Israel, he seizes Jerusalem's temple to serve as the focal point of the new religion that will bring the world together, the new trinity that the world will bow before, and the new commercial force that will have a stranglehold on the commerce and communication of the world. This religion is nothing less than the worship of Satan, who is pictured in Revelation as the dragon; worship of Satan's visible manifestation on earth, the Antichrist; and worship of the Antichrist's chief assistant on earth, the False Prophet (see 2 Thess. 2:3, 4). The temple's use for sacrifices and the observance of holy days will be immediately outlawed (see Dan. 7:25).

These two audacious gambits—the overthrow of Babylon along with the seizing of the temple in Jerusalem make the Antichrist the center of world attention. But he has reached too far.

The Antichrist:
Master of Miscalculation

The Bible is clear: "Pride goes before destruction, and a haughty spirit before a fall" (Prov. 16:18). The greatest human example of this immutable fact will be the Antichrist. From the very beginning, Satan has overestimated his abilities and overreached his boundaries—and the Antichrist follows in the

Evil One's dubious footsteps. After the destruction of the Babylonian system and the seizing of the temple, the Antichrist no doubt will think that accomplishing his objectives will all be downhill from here—coasting to worldwide dominion. And he's right in a way. From here it *is* all downhill—straight to the pit.

By seizing the temple and destroying the Babylonian system, the Antichrist succeeds not in eliminating his enemies but in enraging them and increasing their number. The location of the temple is still the same—smack-dab on the third most holy spot in Islam. So now the Muslims will transfer their hatred and desire for revenge from the Jews to the Antichrist.

But most importantly, the Antichrist's actions will enrage the Jewish people, sparking white-hot fury in the very core of their being by the most appalling of insults to the true God and the temple set apart to the holiness of His name. They will be already disgusted by the Antichrist's failure to honor his treaty with them by coming to their aid when the Kings of the North and South invade. Israel's heart will be already beginning to soften toward the Most High God because of His miraculous intervention to defeat the Kings of the North and South. Now motivated by a combination of fury and zeal, they will turn to their history for guidance and resort to the same measures they took in the times of the Maccabees, but instead of merely waging guerrilla war, they will attempt to assassinate the Antichrist—and they will succeed.

His Descent to Hades

Lulled into a sense of complacency by both his arrogance and the ease of his victories, the Antichrist's security breaks down. An assassin will exploit the opportunity and strike a lethal blow to the head of the Antichrist, a wound so grievous that those attending to him might as well take him directly to the coroner, bypassing the hospital and the EMTs altogether—the Antichrist is dead (see Rev. 13:3). I believe that upon death he will descend directly into Hades or Sheol—the hellish holding tank where those who have rejected the Messiah wait for their ultimate and irreversible consignment to the eternal lake of fire. I believe this is at least part of the reason why the Antichrist is depicted in the book of Revelation as being he who ascends from the Abyss to prevaricate and plunder.

Satan's Offer

Just as Satan took Jesus up into a mountain, showing Him all the kingdoms of the world and offering them as a reward, I believe that Satan may take the Antichrist into the depths of the Abyss and offers him the kingdoms of the world. And while Jesus refused to bow down to Satan, the Antichrist will gladly bow to Satan and worship him. In return for this worship, Satan reanimates the Antichrist, infusing him to the very core of his being with wickedness, rage, and ruthlessness: "Now the beast which I saw was like a leopard, his feet were like the feet of a bear, and his mouth like the mouth of a lion. The dragon gave him his power, his throne, and great authority" (Rev. 13:2).

When the Antichrist ascends from Sheol, his mortal wound miraculously healed, he will fully unveil his worldwide religion. And from this foundation, he will then implement the worldwide system of commerce that becomes the leverage he uses to force the nations of the world to submit to his political control. But first he will capture the imagination and confidence of the world through his miraculous recovery:

> I saw a beast rising up out of the sea, having seven heads and ten horns, and on his horns ten crowns, and on his heads a blasphemous name. . . . The dragon gave him his power, his throne, and great authority. And I saw one of his heads as if it had been mortally wounded, and his deadly wound was healed. And all the world marveled and followed the beast. So they worshiped the dragon who gave authority to the beast; and they worshiped the beast, saying, "Who is like the beast? Who is able to make war with him?" (Rev. 13:1–4)

To the satanically blinded world of the Tribulation, the Antichrist's healing will look exactly like the death and resurrection of Jesus Christ—except in this instance they will see it happen with their own eyes on CNN.

The World's Awe

The Antichrist will capitalize on the world's amazement to point the world to worship not only him, but also the ultimate source of his power—Satan himself. "So they worshiped the dragon [Satan] who gave authority to the beast; and they worshiped the beast" (Rev. 13:4).

Satan is the source of the Antichrist's power, but the Antichrist will delegate this power to a nefarious man designated in Scripture as the "False Prophet." While the Antichrist "was given a mouth to utter proud words and blasphemies" (Rev. 17:5 NIV), the False Prophet will work tirelessly to either persuade or intimidate the world into submission to the Antichrist.

At first appearing as gentle and harmless as a lamb, the False Prophet's mission of persuasion, persecution, and propaganda will reveal his real nature to be the very same as Satan's and the Antichrist's (see Rev. 13:11). But while the Antichrist comes from "the sea," a designation for the Gentile nations, the False Prophet comes from the "the earth," a designation for Israel. Forcing some to worship the Antichrist, he also will convince many others, chiefly relying on the ability given him to perform "great signs, so that he even makes fire come down from heaven on the earth in the sight of men. And he deceives those who dwell on the earth by those signs which he was granted to do in the sight of the beast" (Rev. 13:13–14). Because of the miracles he performs and because he is Jewish, some may believe that the coming attempt to eliminate the Jewish people is in fact a divinely sanctioned fulfillment of Jewish teaching—so great will be the spirit of deception during the Tribulation.

Chief among the seemingly miraculous abilities given to False Prophet is his construction in the temple of an image of the Beast:

> And he [the False Prophet] deceives those who dwell on the earth by those signs which he was granted to do in the sight of the beast, telling those who dwell on the earth to make an image to the beast who was wounded by the sword and lived. He was granted power to give breath to the image of the beast, that the image of the beast should both speak and cause as many as would not worship the image of the beast to be killed. (Rev. 13:14–15)

In other words, this statue—"Terminator 3," if you please—has the ability to discover those who will not worship the satanic trinity and destroy them. Actually, the Scriptures have already given a name to this statue: "the abomination which causes desolation."

Because of the supernatural life-and-death power of this image, it is only a short hop to accomplish another goal of the Antichrist's mission—control of the world's economy: "He [the False Prophet] causes all, both small and great, rich and poor, free and slave, to receive a mark on their right hand or on their foreheads, and that no one may buy or sell except one who has the mark or the name of the beast, or the number of his name" (Rev. 13:16–17). Some people will be persuaded by the False Prophet; some will be eliminated by the False Prophet; some will be intimidated by the False Prophet—but all with the exception of the elect will participate in the system (see Rev. 13:8).

As a result of his mortal wound and his miraculous recovery, the Antichrist, renowned before his assassination as a "man of peace," now becomes the veritable incarnation of Satan. He is the greatest monster the world has ever seen. You could say he's mad as hell at the Jewish people. And his hatred is shared by Satan himself.

Satan: Father of Miscalculation

At the midpoint of the Tribulation, the Antichrist makes his play to control the earth. Simultaneously, Satan makes his play to control heaven. But while the Antichrist appears to be successful at first, Satan's all-out war against the archangel Michael for control of heaven results not only in a stunning defeat, but in banishment from heaven as well:

> "And war broke out in heaven: Michael and his angels fought with the dragon [Satan]; and the dragon and his angels [demons] fought, but they did not prevail, nor was a place found for them in heaven any longer. So the great dragon was cast out, that serpent of old, called the Devil and Satan, who deceives the whole world; he was cast to the earth, and his angels were cast out with him." (Rev. 12:7–9)

Not powerful enough to prevail in heaven, Satan lashes out on the earth against everything God holds dear:

> "Therefore rejoice, O heavens, and you who dwell in them! Woe to the inhabitants of the earth and the sea! For the devil has come down to you, having great wrath, because he knows that he has a short time." Now when the dragon saw that he had been cast to the earth, he persecuted the woman [Israel] who gave birth to the male Child. . . . And the dragon was enraged with the woman, and he went to make war with the rest of her offspring, who keep the commandments of God and have the testimony of Jesus Christ. (Rev. 12:12–13, 17)

Vengeance Against Jews and Christians

With Satan and his angels cast down to earth to join forces with the Antichrist and the False Prophet, the powers of hell will be unfurled on the earth as never before in human history. The objects of their wrath will be the physical seed of Abraham (the Jewish people), and the spiritual seed of Abraham, "[those] who keep the commandments of God and have the testimony of Jesus Christ"—in other words, those who come to know Jesus as their Messiah during the Tribulation.

Satan will target Jews and Christians because attacking them is the only way he can retaliate against God. Unable to prevail against God militarily, Satan will seek revenge against Him by targeting the Jewish people, the apple of God's eye, for extermination. The Antichrist will be similarly motivated, seeking revenge against the Jews who attempted to snuff out his life. All of this will happen at about the same time that the image of the Antichrist is erected in the temple. God's warning to the seed of Abraham in that day is clear—and urgent.

[Jesus said,] "Therefore when you see the 'abomination of desolation,' spoken of by Daniel the prophet, standing in the holy place" (whoever reads, let him understand), "then let those who are in Judea flee to the mountains. Let him who is on the housetop not go down to take anything out of his house. And let him who is in the field not go back to get his clothes. But woe to those who are pregnant and to those who are nursing babies in those days! And pray that your flight may not be in winter or on the Sabbath. For then there will be great tribulation, such as has not been since the beginning of the world until this time, no, nor ever shall be. And unless those days were shortened, no flesh would be saved; but for the elect's sake those days will be shortened." (Matt. 24:15–22)

God will prepare a special place of refuge for His people in the desert. Those who follow the words of Jesus and flee to the desert will be taken care of by God throughout the last half of the Tribulation (see Rev. 12:6).

The desert area of divine protection is identified as Edom, Moab, and Ammon—modern-day Jordan (see Dan. 11:41). Undoubtedly Jordan presently enjoys a more cordial relationship with Israel than any other Arab nation. Interestingly, although the south of Jordan (Edom) will be part of the first Islamic-Russian invasion of the Holy Land, all of Jordan will be spared from the epic battles of the last half of the Tribulation that lead up to the Battle of Armageddon.

Some Christians and Jews who are unable to flee to the Jordanian wilderness will be sheltered from the genocide by caring individuals (see Matt. 25:31–46). Others will be captured and put to death, and these saints will receive a special blessing from God for their courageous devotion to Him in the midst of horrific persecution and torture (see Rev. 14:13).

This time of persecution will last three-and-a-half years, for Daniel 7:21–22, 25 reveals what will happen to the "saints," or the children of Israel during that time:

> As I watched, this horn [the Antichrist] was waging war against the saints [the Jews] and defeating them, until the Ancient of Days came and pronounced judgment in favor of the saints of the Most High, and the time came when they possessed the kingdom [the end of the tribulation period]. . . . He [the Antichrist] will speak against the Most High and oppress his saints and try to change the set times and the laws. The saints will be handed over to him for a time, times, and half a time [the last three and a half years of the Tribulation]. (NIV)

Vindication: The Battle of Armageddon

Just as God removed Satan from the hallowed halls of heaven, He now will begin to dislodge him and his influence from the earth. We often think of the Battle of Armageddon as a short battle that occurs at the end of the Tribulation, but this is only part of the picture. Actually the Battle of Armageddon is a desperate three-and-a-half year campaign by the Antichrist to fend off challenge after challenge to his world rule, culminating in the battle on the plains of Armageddon—the greatest battle ever fought, the most decisive victory ever achieved, and the greatest defeat ever suffered.

There are many reasons why the reign of the satanic trinity will be contentious and short-lived, not the least of which is the curse of God upon their efforts. It is important to realize that the satanic trinity will not dominate the world because of its *power* but instead because of God's *permission*. The Tribulation will last exactly as long as God ordained it to. Satan, the Antichrist, and the False Prophet will stir up exactly as much trouble as God allows them to, and they will experience exactly as much difficulty and frustration as God intends.

Yet there are also three possible reasons from a human point of view why so many are opposed to the rule of the Dragon, the Beast, and the False Prophet. One explanation is the continuing concern of the Muslim world over the desecration of Mount Moriah (the former location of the Dome of the Rock). Another would be that the Antichrist is simply too powerful and too untrustworthy to be allowed to continue to grow in power without a fight. But the explanation that makes the most sense to me is that nations of the world simply do not want the Antichrist to control Middle Eastern oil, and they will do whatever they can to pry his hands off of it. Now these three reasons could all be true, but I believe the last reason will be the most significant one. And so it is in this context that the campaign leading to Armageddon will be set in motion.

The Battle Joined

At the time of the end the king of the South shall attack him [the Antichrist]; and the king of the North shall come against him like a whirlwind, with chariots, horsemen, and with many ships; and he [Antichrist] shall enter the countries, overwhelm them, and pass through. He shall also enter the Glorious Land, and many countries shall be overthrown; but these shall escape from his hand: Edom, Moab, and the prominent people of Ammon. He shall stretch out his hand against the countries, and the land of Egypt shall not escape. He shall have power over the treasures of gold and silver, and over all the precious things of Egypt; also the Libyans and Ethiopians shall follow at his heels. But news from the east and the north shall trouble him; therefore he shall go out with great fury to destroy and annihilate many. And he shall plant the tents of his palace between the seas and the glorious holy mountain [Jerusalem]; yet he shall come to his end, and no one will help him. (Dan. 11:40–45)

This is not the first time we have seen the Kings of the North and the South. This time as before, they represent a resurgent Russian Empire conspiring with a Pan-Islamic Confederation to cleanse Jerusalem and seize control of the oil of the Middle East. Though savaged in battle when they attack Israel, these kings will draw on their vast resources of men and materiel to field a viable fighting force once again—but this time they will have even more help, for fighting beside them this time will be the kings of the East. And this new enemy will disturb the Antichrist very much.

The advancing army of the kings of the East is 200 million strong, marching right through the supernaturally dried bed of the Euphrates River to the very center of the Antichrist's empire. Given these facts, describing the Antichrist as "troubled" is probably a bit of an understatement. Nevertheless, the Antichrist will still take solace in the fact that he has defeated the Kings of the North and South before, and while they may have an extra ally in the form of a confederation of the kings of the East, the Antichrist has three additional allies of his own now as well—Satan; the False Prophet, with his ability to call down fire from heaven; and the image of the Beast, which has the power to destroy those who refuse to obey the Antichrist. So if it's a fight these kings want, it's a fight they'll get.

Why will the "kings from the East," move toward Israel? There are a number of possibilities. First, don't forget how strong Islam is in the East. While the Kings of the North and the South seem to come from Africa, the Middle East, and

Russia, there are many millions of Muslims zealous for their faith living in Afghanistan, Pakistan, India, Malaysia, and Indonesia. Though not part of the first fight to reclaim the holy site of Mount Moriah, they will be no less outraged by its desecration. And perhaps this time Islam will bring all that it has at its disposal to dislodge the blasphemy of the Antichrist from Jerusalem, destroy the third temple, and reconstruct the Dome of the Rock.

Of course the 200 million men could come from the thoroughly secularized and massively populated nation of China, who could also have its own designs on Middle Eastern oil. Japan, secularized, prosperous, and completely dependent on oil imports for the functioning of its economy could certainly play a leadership role in this coming confederation of kings. In any case, I believe that the quest to control Middle Eastern oil is the most likely scenario to drive the kings of the East to the Holy Land. But to control the oil of the Middle East, they must first depose the Antichrist—which means marching on his headquarters in Jerusalem. The Bible itself does not tell us why the "kings of the East" move to confront the Antichrist, only that they will do so.

After hearing the news about the advancing eastern army, the Antichrist will advance from the territory of the twice-defeated King of the South to Armageddon—a natural battlefield—to face the onslaught from the North and East.

Yet as the armies of the world converge upon Armageddon on a massive collision course, suddenly their objective will change. Instead of contending with each other, they will unite to fight the armies of the Messiah that descend from heaven to the storied fields of Armageddon.

The Victory Won

I do not know what will turn these enemy armies into allies united in their commitment to resist the return of the Messiah. Perhaps the Antichrist will remind these armies of what happened to the Kings of the North and the South when they intervened in Israel before. Perhaps the False Prophet will have prophesied this event, predicting a far different outcome than will actually be the case. Whatever the reason, the would-be enemies will be united in their resistance to the Messiah, and united in the destruction they will soon experience.

Armies Defeated. The Second Coming of Jesus Christ to the fields of Armageddon is at once a towering event of human history and the most staggering defeat that any army has ever endured. No one can improve on John's majestic description of this event in Revelation 19:

> I saw heaven standing open and there before me was a white horse, whose rider is called Faithful and True. With justice he judges and makes war. His eyes are like blazing fire, and on his head are many crowns. He has a name written on him that no one but he himself knows. He is dressed in a robe dipped in blood, and his name is the Word of God. The armies of heaven were following him, riding on white horses and dressed in fine linen, white and clean. Out of his mouth comes a sharp sword with which to strike down the nations. "He will rule them with an iron scepter." He treads the winepress of the fury of the wrath of God Almighty. On his robe and on his thigh he has this name written: KING OF KINGS AND LORD OF LORDS.
>
> And I saw an angel standing in the sun, who cried in a loud voice to all the birds flying in midair, "Come, gather together for the great supper of God, so that you may eat the flesh of kings, generals, and mighty men, of horses and their riders, and the flesh of all people, free and slave, small and great."
>
> Then I saw the beast [the Antichrist] and the kings of the earth and their armies gathered together to make war against the rider on the horse and his army [Jesus, his angels, and the saints raptured to heaven at the very beginning of the Tribulation.]. But the beast was captured, and with him the false prophet who had performed the miraculous signs on his behalf. With these signs he had deluded those who had received the mark of the beast and worshiped his image. The two of them

were thrown alive into the fiery lake of burning sulfur. The rest of them were killed with the sword that came out of the mouth of the rider on the horse, and all the birds gorged themselves on their flesh. (vv. 11–21 NIV)

John writes that Christ had a name "written on him that no one but he himself knows." As a Jew, John remembers that God appeared to Abraham, Isaac, and Jacob by the name of God Almighty, *El Shaddai*. But He did not reveal Himself to them by the name of Jehovah *(Yahweh)* (see Exodus 6:3). The patriarchs knew God as the Almighty One, but they had no concept of Him as an intimate friend and master—the One who delights to walk with His children "in the cool of the day." But Christ's robe, dipped in His spotless blood shed on the cross, is His prayer shawl, and upon this shawl is written KING OF KINGS AND LORD OF LORDS.

John wrote that Christ's name was written on His thigh. You may be wondering how anything could be written on a man's thigh and be visible to passersby. As the corners of His prayer shawl rest on his thighs, the name of Jehovah God will be spelled out on each of the shawl's four corners with the unique coils and knots of the *tzitzit,* which is Hebrew for "fringes." Thus on his robe and on his prayer shawl He wears the name "Lord."

The prophet Zechariah adds to the description of this longed-for day, when those martyred for their testimony are vindicated as God lays waste His foes:

A day of the LORD is coming . . . I will gather all the nations to Jerusalem to fight against it; the city will be captured, the houses ransacked, and the women raped. Half of the city will go into exile, but the rest of the people will not be taken from the city.

Then the LORD will go out and fight against those nations, as he fights in the day of battle. On that day his feet will stand on the Mount of Olives, east of Jerusalem, and the Mount of Olives will be split in two from east to west, forming a great valley, with half of the mountain moving north and half moving south. You will flee by my mountain valley, for it will extend to Azel. . . . Then the LORD my God will come, and all the holy ones with him.

On that day there will be no light, no cold or frost. It will be a unique day, without daytime or nighttime—a day known to the Lord. When evening comes, there will be light.

On that day living water will flow out from Jerusalem, half to the eastern sea [the Dead Sea] and half to the western sea [the Mediterranean], in summer and in winter.

The LORD will be king over the whole earth. On that day there will be one LORD, and his name the only name.

The whole land, from Geba to Rimmon, south of Jerusalem, will become like the Arabah [wilderness, or desert]. But Jerusalem will be raised up and remain in its place, from the Benjamin Gate to the site of the First Gate, to the Corner Gate, and from the Tower of Hananel to the royal winepresses. It will be inhabited; never again will it be destroyed. Jerusalem will be secure.

This is the plague with which the LORD will strike all the nations that fought against Jerusalem: Their flesh will rot while they are still standing on their feet, their eyes will rot in their sockets, and their tongues will rot in their mouths. (14:1–12 NIV)

The battle over Jerusalem is part of the battle of Armageddon, a confrontation so encompassing that soldiers will cover the land like locusts, from the plains of Meggido north of Palestine, through the valley of Jehoshaphat near Jerusalem, and on down to the land of Edom to the south and east of Jerusalem.

Revelation 14:20 declares that the blood from this battle will rise "up to the horses' bridles" for a distance of 1600 furlongs, approximately two hundred miles. And if you measure from the northern part of Palestine to the southern boundaries described in this prophecy, you'll discover that the distance is approximately two hundred miles.[1]

Armageddon, the world's most natural battlefield, will be bathed in blood. The Bible has predicted it, down to the length of the battlefield. Mark my words, this battle of unsurpassed carnage is not a fable, it is a fact—and every tick of the clock brings us closer to it.

The crowning event of this battle occurs when the Antichrist, who believes he can defeat God Almighty, will gather his forces to face a heavenly army led by the Messiah Himself. He will be done with shaking his fist in the face of God; his boastful, deceitful tongue will be silenced forever. The Scripture tells us, "But the beast was captured, and with him the false prophet who had performed the miraculous signs on his behalf. With these signs he had deluded those who had received the mark of the beast and worshiped his image. The two of them were thrown alive into the fiery lake of burning sulfur" (Rev. 19:20 NIV). The victory is the Lord's!

Israel Protected. Not only will the armies of the world be defeated, but the Jewish people—the object of God's loyal covenant love—will be protected.

One of the most commonly ignored biblical truths is this: what a nation or an individual does to the nation of Israel is what God repays to them. God couldn't have been more clear: "I will bless those who bless you, and I will curse him who curses you" (Gen. 12:3).

The Antichrist will track down, torment, and attempt to annihilate Israel; in return, God will track down, torment, and annihilate him from the face of the earth. The true Messiah will come, bringing the armies of heaven with him, and the Antichrist and his forces will be demolished.

If you doubt this principle from the Word of God, consider this: Once I was standing at Checkpoint Charlie at the divide separating West and East Berlin. I had been invited to Germany to speak to the United States military and was taking a few hours to look around. Our West German guide asked me,

"Pastor Hagee, why do you think God permitted the communists to build a wall around us?"

The answer came to me instantly because the day before I had visited Dachau. "Because your parents built a wall around the Jews in Dachau and Auschwitz," I answered. "Just look at this wall. It's twelve feet high, just like the one at Dachau. It's electrified at the bottom, just like the one at Dachau. It has machine gun towers down the middle, just like the one at Dachau. It has killer dogs roaming in between the inner and outer walls, just like the one at Dachau. Everything your parents did to the Jewish people, son, the communists are doing to you."

You'll find this principle illustrated from the Scriptures in the story of the Passover: Pharaoh instructed the midwives of Egypt to kill male Jewish children. When Israel left Egypt, God killed the firstborn child in every Egyptian family (see Exodus 1:15–16; 4:22; and 11:5).

The Reconciliation Complete

Ah, my friend, I want you to know that I expect Him to appear twice in the days ahead: the first time only for an instant to protect the Church, His Bride, from the wrath of the Tribulation by removing her from the earth before it begins. But He will also appear on earth a second time as well. Jesus Christ will step down from heaven and place his foot on the Mount of Olives. He will win the battle for Jerusalem and Israel. In the aftermath of this battle, His people will finally understand who He really is and what He has come to offer them. The hearts of the Jewish people—warmed toward God because of His intervention to defeat the Russian-Islamic coalition, will now turn fully to their true God: "And I will pour on the house of David and on the inhabitants of Jerusalem the Spirit of grace and supplication; then they will look on Me whom they pierced. Yes, they will mourn for Him as one mourns for his only son, and grieve for Him as one grieves for a firstborn" (Zech. 12:10). And in that moment, the blindness of the Jewish people toward their Messiah will be taken away and they will be saved:

> For I do not desire, brethren, that you should be ignorant of this mystery, lest you should be wise in your own opinion, that blindness in part has happened to Israel until the fullness of the Gentiles has come in. And so all Israel will be saved, as it is written: "The Deliverer will come out of Zion, and He will turn away ungodliness from Jacob; for this is My covenant with them, when I take away their sins." Concerning the gospel they are enemies for your sake, but concerning the election they are beloved for the sake of the fathers. For the gifts and the calling of God are irrevocable. For as you were once disobedient to God, yet have now obtained mercy through their disobedience, even so these also have now been disobedient, that through the mercy shown you they also may obtain mercy. For God has committed them all to disobedience, that He might have mercy on all. Oh, the depth of the riches both of the wisdom and knowledge of God! How unsearchable are His judgments and His ways past finding out! "For who has known the mind of the LORD? Or who has become His counselor?" "Or who has first given to Him and it shall be repaid to him?" For of Him and through Him and to Him are all things, to whom be glory forever. Amen. (Rom. 11:25–36)

Jerusalem's Rebirth

Of whom was Zechariah speaking when he wrote,

> "'Sing and rejoice, O daughter of Zion! For behold, I am coming and I will dwell in your midst,' says the LORD. 'Many nations shall be joined to the LORD in that day, and they shall become My people. And I will dwell in your midst. Then you will know that the LORD of hosts has sent Me to you. And the LORD will take possession of Judah as His inheritance in the Holy Land, and will again choose Jerusalem'" (2:10–12)

The apostle Paul wrote "here we do not have an enduring city, but we are looking for the city that is to come" (Heb.

13:14 NIV). Jerusalem has existed for at least three thousand years; she is holy to Jews, Christians, and Muslims. Throughout history, she has been targeted for conquest many times, and by many nations: Babylon in 586 B.C., Rome in 63 B.C., the Muslims in A.D. 637, the Crusaders in A.D. 1099, and the Muslims again in A.D. 1187. During the Arab-Israeli Wars (pre-1967), the city was divided; the Old City was retained by Jordan and the New City became the capital of Israel. But in the 1967 Six-Day War, Israel captured the Old City and formally annexed it as her own.

But what does Jerusalem's future hold? The Bible has much to say about David's City of God: "On that day living water will flow out from Jerusalem, half to the eastern sea [the Dead Sea] and half to the western sea [the Mediterranean], in summer and in winter" (Zech. 14:8 NIV). The lifeless Dead Sea will live for the first time since Creation, connecting through Jerusalem to the Mediterranean.

"The LORD will be king over the whole earth. On that day there will be one LORD, and his name the only name" (Zech. 14:9 NIV). Jerusalem will be the capital city from which Jesus Christ will reign over the entire earth.

"The whole land, from Geba to Rimmon, south of Jerusalem, will become like the Arabah. But Jerusalem will be raised up and remain in its place, from the Benjamin Gate to the site of the First Gate, to the Corner Gate, and from the Tower of Hananel to the royal winepresses. It will be inhabited; never again will it be destroyed. Jerusalem will be secure" (Zech. 14:10, 11 NIV). The environs around Jerusalem will be transformed into a broad, low valley, like the Arabah. This will both make Jerusalem stand out and make the surrounding areas more fertile.[2]

The New Jerusalem

The true Messiah, Jesus Christ, upon His return from Heaven and victory over the satanic trinity, will rule from Jerusalem in the Millennium—the thousand-year reign of God upon the earth. For the first time in centuries, Jerusalem will not fear her enemies. And after the Millennium, when Satan and his followers have been eternally banished to the lake of fire, God will destroy this present world. He will then present us with a new heaven and a new earth, to which a New Jerusalem will descend.

> Then I saw a new heaven and a new earth, for the first heaven and the first earth had passed away, and there was no longer any sea. I saw the Holy City, the new Jerusalem, coming down out of heaven from God, prepared as a bride beautifully dressed for her husband. And I heard a loud voice saying, "Now the dwelling of God is with men, and he will live with them. They will be his people, and God himself will be with them and be their God. He will wipe every tear from their eyes. There will be no more death or mourning or crying or pain, for the old order of things has passed away." . . .
>
> One of the seven angels who had the seven bowls full of the seven last plagues came and said to me, "Come, I will show you the bride, the wife of the Lamb." And he carried me away in the Spirit to a mountain great and high, and showed me the Holy City, Jerusalem, coming down out of heaven from God. It shone with the glory of God, and its brilliance was like that of a very precious jewel, like a jasper, clear as crystal. It had a great, high wall with twelve gates, and with twelve angels at the gates. On the gates were written the names of the twelve tribes of Israel. There were three gates on the east, three on the north, three on the south and three on the west. The wall of the city had twelve foundations, and on them were the names of the twelve apostles of the Lamb.
>
> The angel who talked with me had a measuring rod of gold to measure the city, its gates and its wall. The city was laid out like a square, as long as it was wide. He measured the city with the rod and found it to be 12,000 stadia [about 1400 miles] in length, and as wide and high as it is long. He measured its wall and it was 144 cubits [about 200 feet] thick, by man's measurement, which the angel was using. The wall was made of jasper, and the city of pure gold, as pure as glass. The foundations of

the city walls were decorated with every kind of precious stone. The first foundation was jasper, the second sapphire, the third chalcedony, the fourth emerald, the fifth sardonyx, the sixth carnelian, the seventh chrysolite, the eighth beryl, the ninth topaz, the tenth chrysoprase, the eleventh jacinth, and the twelfth amethyst. The twelve gates were twelve pearls, each gate made of a single pearl. The street of the city was of pure gold, like transparent glass.

I did not see a temple in the city, because the Lord God Almighty and the Lamb are its temple. The city does not need the sun or the moon to shine on it, for the glory of God gives it light, and the Lamb is its lamp. The nations will walk by its light, and the kings of the earth will bring their splendor into it. On no day will its gates ever be shut, for there will be no night there. The glory and honor of the nations will be brought into it. Nothing impure will ever enter it, nor will anyone who does what is shameful or deceitful, but only those whose names are written in the Lamb's book of life.

The angel showed me the river of the water of life, as clear as crystal, flowing from the throne of God and of the Lamb down the middle of the great street of the city. On each side of the river stood the tree of life, bearing twelve crops of fruit, yielding its fruit every month. And the leaves of the tree are for the healing of the nations. No longer will there be any curse. The throne of God and of the Lamb will be in the city, and his servants will serve him. They will see his face, and his name will be on their foreheads. There will be no more night. They will not need the light of a lamp or the light of the sun, for the Lord God will give them light. And they will reign for ever and ever. (Rev. 21:1–4, 9–26; 22:1–5 NIV)

What a glorious picture! Jerusalem, which has endured so much suffering, will be magnificently redeemed! The Bible tells us that by faith Abraham looked forward to the New Jerusalem of eternity, "the city which has foundations, whose builder and maker is God" (Heb. 11:10). Many of the Old Testament saints longed for the New Jerusalem, "therefore God is not ashamed to be called their God, for he has prepared a city for them" (Heb. 11:16).

Soon and Very Soon

As I write this, my heart is warmed by the realization that Jerusalem, the united capital of the Jewish homeland, is celebrating her three thousandth anniversary this year. I'm planning to visit that beloved city during her celebration, but as I walk down those cobbled roads I know my thoughts will turn from the sights before me to things that happened centuries ago—and things sure to take place in the not-too-distant future.

When I stand outside Jerusalem, I will remember what Jesus said when the Pharisees tried to keep Him away from the city, warning Him darkly of plots to assassinate Him: "Jesus told them, . . . I will drive out demons and heal people today and tomorrow, and on the third day I will reach my goal" (Luke 13:32 NIV). That is a prophetic statement as well as a historic one. The psalmist wrote that a thousand years in God's sight are like a day that has just gone by, as a mere watch in the night (see Ps. 90:4).

A thousand years is as a day. Today and tomorrow—two days. Two thousand years. The power of the Gospel has covered the earth, and on the third day the Messiah will be glorified in his thousand-year reign on earth, the Millennium. We are coming to the end of the second day. And the third day is forming just below the horizon; it will dawn with the appearing of Messiah, *Mashiach,* the Anointed One who will be sent by God to inaugurate the final redemption at the end of days.

What then shall we do?

As the Apostle Peter wrote: "And so we have the prophetic word confirmed, which you do well to heed as a light that shines in a dark place, until the day dawns and the morning star rises in your hearts; knowing this first, that no prophecy of Scripture is of any private interpretation, for prophecy never came by the will of man, but holy men of God spoke as they were moved by the Holy Spirit" (2 Pet. 1:19–21).

Peter testified in this passage that the accounts of the life, miracles, ministry, death, and resurrection of Jesus Christ are not the product of cunning fables. Peter and the other disciples saw Jesus. They touched him, ate with him, talked to him— they even saw him ascend into heaven. They were *eyewitnesses* of his majesty. And so Peter says "we have the prophetic word *confirmed*." Peter himself, a Jewish man well-acquainted with the writings of the prophets, saw how the Lord Jesus fulfilled the prophecies of the Old Testament. And he was convinced that just as Jesus fulfilled the prophecies concerning His first coming, so too would Jesus fulfill the prophecies of the times yet to come.

My friends, if you remember nothing else about this book, please grasp with your head and your heart this overpowering truth from the Word of God—we are the terminal generation. We are the ones who need to prepare today for our ever after. Like no other generation, we are the ones who cannot take for granted tomorrow. We must not put off until tomorrow spiritual decisions and spiritual actions which can be done today.

If you are a believer in Jesus the Messiah, lift up your head and rejoice, for your redemption is drawing near. Too many Christians are living as if they're going to be here forever. To them the words of Jesus shine like a warning beacon: "And this gospel of the kingdom will be preached in all the world as a witness to all the nations, and then the end will come" (Matt. 24:14).

If you have yet to trust Jesus Christ as Messiah, the signs of the times should compel you to recognize that the hand of God is moving in the city of Jerusalem and in the nation of Israel. Messiah is soon to come. If you listen closely, you can hear the footsteps of Messiah walking through the clouds of heaven. You can hear the thundering hoofbeats of the four horsemen of the Apocalypse as even now they pick up speed, racing to their rendezvous with destiny on the fields of Armageddon.

If this book outlives my time on earth, and I honestly believe it will, let me assure you that it is not too late to recognize Jesus Christ as the Son of God, the promised Messiah. He is truly King of Kings and Lord of Lords; and He wants to bring you life abundant on earth and life eternal in the world to come. He extends to you the opportunity to escape the coming time of trial.

Like the two-faced Janus of old, Israel will soon see the advent of two Messiahs: one false, one true.

Which one will you choose?

Notes

Chapter 1

1. Reuters Newmedia, "Arab Leaders Flock to Rabin Funeral," 6 November 1995.
2. Reuters NewMedia, "Israel Lays Rabin to Rest," 6 November 1995.
3. Ibid.
4. Michael Chute, "Jim Henry Attends Rabin Funeral; Says World 'Galvanized' for Peace," Baptist Press. [no date given]
5. Rabbi Eliezer Waldman, Rosh Yeshiva, Yeshivat Kiryat Arba, "Analysis of a Tragedy: From the Pain Must Come Renewed Dedication Toward Rebuilding Jewish Life with Unconditional Love for our Fellow Jew," November 1995. Also, a survey conducted by Gallup Israel on May during May 22–28 on behalf of the Israel/Palestine Center for Research and Information revealed the following on Israeli attitudes toward Jerusalem:

- Less than ⅔ (65%) of the Israeli Jewish adult public voiced full support for exclusive Israeli sovereignty over all of Jerusalem.
- Only 8% of the Israeli Jewish adult public believe that the Palestinians will accept the solution of exclusive Israeli sovereignty over all of Jerusalem.
- 28% of the Israeli Jewish adult public is ready to accept the solution of divided sovereignty whereby Israel will have sovereignty over all of West Jerusalem and the Jewish neighborhoods in East Jerusalem, while the Palestinians will have sovereignty over the Arab parts of East Jerusalem.

- 25% of the Israeli Jewish adult public believe that the Palestinians will accept the option of Israeli sovereignty over all of West Jerusalem and the Jewish neighborhoods in East Jerusalem, while the Palestinians will have sovereignty over the Arab parts of East Jerusalem.
- 56% of the Israeli Jewish adult public believe that the Palestinians will only settle for exclusive Palestinian sovereignty over East Jerusalem on the basis of the June 4, 1967 lines.
- 3% of the Israeli Jewish adult public support joint Israeli-Palestinian undivided sovereignty over all of Jerusalem.
- 3% of the Israeli Jewish adult public support the internationalization of the city under the United Nations.

6. Tom Hundley and Storer H. Rowley, "Israelis Again Rally for Peace," *Chicago Tribune,* 13 November 1995.

7. Reuters NewMedia, "Stunned Israel to Continue Rabin's Peace Policy," 5 November 1995.

8. Reuters NewMedia, "Jordan's King Invokes Martyrdom," 6 November 1995.

9. Reuters NewMedia, "Clinton Urges Israelis to Follow Rabin Path," 6 November 1995.

10. Serge Schmemann, *New York Times* News Service, 18 December 1995. It is nevertheless important to recognize that as of December 1995, most Israelis are not in favor of surrendering the Golan Heights—regardless of how much the current Israeli government is willing to deal. Here's what the polls reveal:

Do you believe that the President of Syria wants to reach a true peace with Israel?

Yes 46%

No 48%

No reply 6%

Are you for or against full withdrawal from the Golan in return for full peace with Syria and appropriate security arrangements?

For 42%

Against 55%

No reply 3%

The Dahaf Institute survey was carried out for "Yediot Ahronot" on Tuesday and Wednesday 12–13 December and covered 503 who are a representative sample of the adult population in the country. The standard error is + / − 4 percent. (Published in "Yediot Ahronot" on December 15, 1995.)

Are you for or against withdrawal from the Golan Heights in return for a full peace agreement with Syria, on the terms of the agreements which were signed with Egypt and Jordan?

For 35%

Against 46%

Don't know 12%

Refuse to reply 7%

The "Mutagim" survey was carried out for "Maariv" on Wednesday, December 13, and covered a sample of 536 interviewees from the adult Jewish population in the country. The standard error is + / − 4.5 percent. (Published in "Maariv" December 15, 1995.)

11. Ibid.

12. Reuters NewMedia, "Israeli Student Confesses to Killing Rabin," 6 November 1995.

Chapter 2

1. Noam M. M. Neusner, "Saving Faith," *The Tampa Tribune,* 10 December 1995.

2. Storer H. Rowley, "Probe Divides Israel's Self-Image," *Chicago Tribune,* 28 November 1995.

3. Ibid.

4. Quoted in Rowley, "Israel's Self-Image."

5. Tom Hundley, "Beyond Rabin: Life in Israel Has Been Changing for Years," *Chicago Tribune,* 12 November 1995.

6. Neusner, "Saving Faith."

7. Hundley, "Beyond Rabin."

8. Jerry Adler and Jeffrey Bartholet, "Souls at War," *Newsweek,* 20 November 1995, 59.

9. Quoted in Adler and Bartholet, "Souls at War," 59.

10. Union of Rabbis for Eretz Yisrael, "Leading Rabbis from Israel and the Diaspora Held a Conference at the Ramada Renaissance Hotel, Jerusalem, on the 27th Day of Heshvan 5754," *Jerusalem One,* 11 November 1993.

11. Steven Emerson, "A Look Inside the Radical Islamist Network," *The New Republic,* 12 June 1995.

12. Quoted in Emerson, "The Radical Islamist Network."

13. Ibid.

14. Ibid.

15. Ibid.

16. Ibrahim Sarbal, leader of the Islamic Jihad Movement in Palestine—al Aqsa Brigades. Quote is provided by the Anti-Defamation League of B'nai B'rith.

17. Quote is provided by the Anti-Defamation League of B'nai B'rith.

18. Amos Oz, "Israelis Will Not Stand for Fanaticism," *Newsweek,* 20 November 1995.

19. Esquiu, Buenos Aires, 21 March 1971.

20. Speech given in Teheran, Associated Press, 19 February 1979.

21. Michael Horowitz, "New Intolerance Between Crescent and Cross," *Wall Street Journal,* 5 July 1995.

22. Ibid.

23. Marty Croll, "Israel Asks: Where Is Peace?" *Baptist Press.*

24. "Israelis Appeal for Unity," *The Tampa Tribune,* 11 December 1995.

25. Ibid.

Chapter 3

1. J. Dwight Pentecost, *Things to Come* (Grand Rapids, MI: Zondervan, 1958), 320.

2. William Kelly, *Notes on Daniel* (New York: Loizeaux Brothers), 50.

3. Charles H. Dyer and Angela Elwell Hunt, *The Rise of Babylon* (Wheaton, IL: Tyndale, 1991), 116.

4. Ibid., 107.

Chapter 4

1. Frank S. Mead, ed., *The Encyclopedia of Religious Quotations* (Old Tappan, NJ: Revell, 1965), 34.

2. Hank Hanegraaff, "Fulfilled Prophecy As an Apologetic," *Christian Research Journal* (Fall 1989):7.

3. Ibid.

4. Ibid.

5. Ibid.

6. Floyd Hamilton, *The Basis of Christian Faith* (New York: Harper and Row, 1964), 160.

7. John F. Walvoord and Roy B. Zuck, eds., *The Bible Knowledge Commentary, New Testament Edition* (Wheaton, IL: Victor Books, 1983), 21.

8. John F. Walvoord and Roy B. Zuck, eds., *The Bible Knowledge Commentary, Old Testament Edition* (Wheaton, IL: Victor Books, 1985), 873.

9. Footnote for Isaiah 9:1, *The NIV Study Bible, 10th Anniversary Edition* (Grand Rapids, MI: Zondervan, 1995), 1023.

Chapter 5

1. "Doomsday Clock Reset," *Tampa Tribune,* 9 December 1995.

2. Richard Preston, *The Hot Zone* (New York: Random House, 1994), 20.

3. Ibid., 46.

4. Dr. Aaron Lerner, Associate, Independent Media Review and Analysis, "Golan Facts and Myths."

5. Ibid.

6. John Wesley White, *Thinking the Unthinkable* (Orlando: Creation House, 1992), 35.

7. Ibid.

8. Alan Unterman, *Dictionary of Jewish Lore and Legend* (New York: Thames and Hudson, 1991), 72.

9. "Experts Warn of Threat Posed by Reinvigorated Diseases," *AIDS Weekly Plus,* 7 August 1995, 13–14.

10. "Living Longer with AIDS: The True Cost," *AIDS Weekly Plus,* 31 July 1995, 31.

11. Gordon Lindsay, *Forty Signs of the Soon Coming of Christ* (Dallas: Christ for the Nations, 1969), 20.

12. U.S. Geological Survey National Earthquake Information Center, "Frequency of Occurrence of Earthquakes." They note, "As more and more seismographs are installed in the world, more earthquakes can be and have been located. However, the number of large earthquakes (magnitude 6.0 or greater) have stayed relatively constant. Note, in fact, that the last decade has produced substantially fewer large earthquakes than show in the long-term averages." Nevertheless,

it is true that the Bible predicts that earthquakes *will* increase in the last days, and the number of earthquakes measured has increased 1.58 times between 1983 and 1992.

Chapter 6

1. Population statistics from *The 1995 CIA World Fact Book*.

Chapter 7

1. To be sure, as the people of formerly communist countries face the hardships involved in modernizing their economy, they long for aspects of their former life. And so communists (usually reborn as free-market capitalists) are sometimes elected to political office. Memory is like that: the people remember the days when they could afford food and rent—and they forget that while the necessities were affordable, they couldn't buy anything because the shelves of their stores were bare and that they waited for years and years before an apartment became available for rent.

2. Quoted in Henry H. Halley, *Halley's Bible Handbook* (Grand Rapids, MI: Zondervan, 1962), 18.

3. Douglas MacArthur, Address to a Joint Meeting of Congress, 19 April 1951.

4. "What Rights Are Being Trounced Upon Here?" *Rocky Mountain News*, 9 December 1995.

5. Quoted in Don Feder, *Pagan America* (Lafayette, LA: Huntington House, 1993), 134.

6. Quoted in a press release from the Christian Coalition on December 22, 1995. It goes on to say, in part, "After Christian Coalition contacted NPR executive producer Ellen Weiss, Weiss admitted that Codrescu's commentary 'crossed the line.' When Christian Coalition pressed NPR to make a public apology, Weiss initially declined, but contacted Christian Coalition late yesterday evening and said an apology may be forthcoming on today's broadcast [and in fact 30 seconds were devoted to an apology on December 22]. No punitive action is planned against Codrescu. NPR declined to allow Christian Coalition Executive Director Ralph Reed two minutes of air time on 'All Things Considered' to offer an opposing view. . . . 'This is one more example of religious bigotry subsidized with tax dollars,' said Ralph Reed. 'We have long passed the time for full privatization of

National Public Radio. These attacks on people of faith must end.'"
And they will—when Messiah comes.

7. *Las Posadas* is the Mexican version of the search for the Christ child.

8. Quoted in Halley, *Halley's Bible Handbook,* 19.

9. Ibid., 18.

Chapter 8

1. Quoted in John Wesley White, *The Coming World Dictator* (Minneapolis: Bethany Fellowship, 1981), 21.

2. Much of this information comes from the Golan Heights Information Server on the World Wide Web. For more information, or to help, contact:

The Golan Residents Committee (GRC)
P.O. Box 67
Qazrin 12900, Israel
E-mail: golan-r@golan.org.il
Mailing list: golan-h@golan.org.il
Telephone: (+972)-6-962966/77
Fax: (+972)-6-962429
Web: http://www.golan.org.il/

3. The United Nations Disengagement Force is headquartered in Damascus, Syria. Currently about 1,031 troops, assisted by the military observers of UNTSO's Observer Group Golan, patrol the area of separation. The force has suffered thirty-seven fatalities in the course of its mission. See the U.N. Web page for more information (http://www.CAM.ORG/~sac/SACIS).

4. Tom Hundley and Storer Rowley, "Israelis Again Rally for Peace," *Chicago Tribune,* 13 November 1995.

5. "World Waits to See If Peace Process Will Survive," *The Orlando Sentinel,* 5 November 1995.

6. For more information about the Islamic Association for Palestine, access their Web page at http://www.io.org/~iap/.

7. Chaim Richman, "What Is the Temple Institute?" To find out more about the work of the Temple Institute, Jerusalem, and the Temple, send an email message at crlight@netvision.net.il, or fax: Rabbi Chaim Richman, 972-2-860-453.

8. Imam Sheik Ahmad Ibrahim, HAMAS leader, in a sermon at the Palestine Mosque in Gaza. Quote is provided by the Anti-Defamation League of the B'nai B'rith.

9. The Islamic Association for Palestine, "Did You Know?: Basic Facts about the Palestine Problem," as found on their Web site at http://www.io.org/~iap/.

10. Walvoord and Zuck, *The Bible Knowledge Commentary, Old Testament Edition,* 1299–1300.

11. Note that renowned evangelical scholar Edwin Yamauchi suspects that Magog is located in Turkey, while Charles Dyer believes that the far north "probably" encompasses "the land bridge between the Black and Caspian Seas."

12. Walvoord and Zuck, *The Bible Knowledge Commentary, Old Testament Edition,* 1300.

13. *New York Times,* 31 December 1995, Editorial Section.

Chapter 9

1. J. Dwight Pentecost, *Prophecy for Today* (Grand Rapids, MI: Zondervan, 1961), 142.

2. Walvoord and Zuck, *The Bible Knowledge Commentary, Old Testament Edition,* 1571.